BIG
LITTLE
SHIFTS

A PRACTITIONER'S GUIDE TO COMPLEXITY
FOR ORGANISATIONAL CHANGE AND ADAPTATION

Dr Josie McLean

First edition, 2020

ISBN: 978-0-6488650-0-1 (paperback)

ISBN: 978-0-6488650-1-8 (ePub)

The Partnership Pty. Ltd.
PO Box 192
Blackwood 5051
South Australia
Australia

www.the-partnership.com.au

NATIONAL
LIBRARY
OF AUSTRALIA

A catalogue record for this work is available from the National Library of Australia

Dedication

This book was written during the summer of 2019–20 in Australia. It was a summer characterised by major bush fires in all states, but particularly in the south eastern portion of Australia. Lives and livelihoods have been lost. The full cost is incalculable.

The summer, droughts, fires, water shortages, fish kills and then floods, was an awakening for the Australian public with regard to the immediacy of climate change. It was followed quickly by the novel Coronavirus global pandemic. I am finishing this book just as we are easing lockdown restrictions during May in Australia and feeling the uncertainty of the economic damage done in addition to the knowledge that 'normal' is unlikely to ever return.

Adequately responding to climate change, still a stronger threat than the pandemic, will demand deeper cultural changes within society, businesses and enterprises of all sorts as we come to appreciate the true complexity of the challenge and learn more about how to meet that complexity.

I dedicate this book about how to influence organisational adaptation and change in complexity to every firefighter, health care worker and self-inspired volunteer. You are demonstrating what distributed leadership and emergent action looks like within a living system.

Thank you.

Acknowledgements

I want to acknowledge and thank all who have inspired my learning and subsequently, this book. Some CEOs, in particular, have offered me unique opportunities to play within their organisations. I do not mean that flippantly; I mean that they have allowed me to experiment and learn about the transition we will be exploring. Some CEOs have not enabled the experimental space, and I have learned a great deal from those experiences too. To all the managers, team leaders and people that I have come into contact with in either coaching or leadership programs – I thank you. You have educated me!

I also wish to thank my colleague Dr Sam Wells as we explored the theory in action – often together. His enormous conceptual capacity is matched by his humanity.

In addition, my thinking of course stands upon the shoulders of some seriously big thinkers – many of whom I have had the privilege of working with in person. My major influences have been Donella Meadows, Peter Senge, Margaret Wheatley, Fritjof Capra, Ronald Heifetz and Dexter Dunphy. I have cited these authors directly where relevant so that you can follow your own trail of learning too.

Finally, I wish to acknowledge the time writing this book has taken and the understanding and support that has been provided by my husband Duart. No greater love hath a man than to encourage his wife to author a book!

Thank you.

Leadership during crisis

I completed the first draft of this book as the bushfires raged in Australia during the summer of 2019-20. Who knew that at that very moment, the seeds of a global transformation were already taking root in a place that few of us had previously heard of – Wuhan, China? This prologue aims to acknowledge the recent world changing events, make links between it and the content, and add some relevant thoughts about leading change during a crisis.

The Coronavirus/COVID-19 pandemic has only made the contents of this book even more relevant. I am not expecting that we will 'snap back' to pre-pandemic conditions at all. Even though the lure of the familiar will be very strong, going backwards in time is not possible (with current technology at least). The changes made in response to the immediate threat that this virus poses to our societies have been pervasive and deep. The adaptations have challenged us as social beings used to touching each other and being in the company of others. These big little shifts, small changes to the simple rules at the heart of our cultures (identified in Chapter 4) have catalysed major emergent changes across many systems. Major systems such as politics, health, employment, transport, education, technology, and even our natural environment. We are experiencing a 'whole systems change'. How long will we need to continue living like this? What will be the long term effects of these adaptations we have made? Time will tell, but the theory would suggest that we can expect the legacy of these days will live on.

As I write, a vaccine is not yet visible on the immediate time horizon and many of us are living in 'lockdown' – isolating ourselves to suppress the transmission of the virus within our societies. Some countries and communities are proving more successful at this strategy that others. The stimulus to change provided by the virus, brings the values at the heart of adaptive change into stark relief (Chapter 7, Element 3). Do we value our health system and people's lives more than the economy? Is the choice as stark as that? Some countries, such as the USA seem to believe that it's not a clear cut choice. Some argue that a weakened economy will also cost lives and that argument is made within the context of that country's history, cultural preferences for individual liberty, and much weaker social welfare nets. In Australia, the response has been very different. We have seen the Australian federal government form a national cabinet with state government leaders to create a united approach – but one that may be applied with local nuances within the context of each state. Weighing up the values of life versus economy, Australia has clearly chosen lives. The governments have used their authority to put in place social distancing restrictions. And even in the process of distancing, values were clarified in a short period of time, as people developed a preference for the term 'physical distancing' to make it clear that we humans all need and continue to desire social contact.

Using what we already know in an emergency

During the initial stages of the pandemic, a focus of leadership during a crisis has emerged. An emergency requires action with clear direction, comforting confidence, clear communication and messages. The clear direction comes from what we already know. Within this book, I draw on Heifetz, Grashow & Linsky's (2009) terminology of a 'technical challenge' (Chapter 7, Element 2). An emergency is initially technical and the authority figure uses a great deal of 'telling'. The telling within the context of an emergency however, needs to be undertaken with empathy. An understanding of what people are experiencing, and communicating with them through that understanding. New Zealand's Prime Minister, Jacinda Ardern has become the textbook example of how to do this well. Perhaps she has learned from vast experience – she has lead her country through three major emergencies during her first term as PM. If you haven't watched Ardern's Facebook live video chat with her nation as they all prepared to 'hunker down' for four weeks, I highly recommend it. She is demonstrating the provision of the 'services of authority' (identified in Chapter 5) to her people with tremendous poise.

The period of emergency will last for varying amounts of time. During this time, the whole system experiences a heightened sense of stress and distress as immediate changes are put into place. Those changes may be single- or double-loop changes (Chapter 3).

In the longer term though, double-loop changes or adaptation will be required, where we examine the assumptions we have made and ask if they remain relevant within our changed context. The stress in the system is still high, although it is reducing as we become accustomed to our new realities. Sir Winston Churchill, Prime Minister of Britain during World War 2 is often quoted as having said, "never let a good crisis go to waste". During a crisis, change agents have the opportunity for radical, transformation; triple-loop change. A transformation of this type is rarely seen despite many books and consultants talking about transformational change. Transformation is currently more possible because of the extent of whole systems change already caused by the response to the pandemic – the larger system is already disturbed and ripe for further paradigm shifting change.

Transformative possibilities come after the emergency

The disruption is also being fuelled by the pause on life as we know it. It is being generated by the lockdowns. Anecdotally, as I speak with clients online, it seems that many are beginning to ask themselves, 'how do I really want to live'? The virus has shone a spotlight on many facets of the broader system that are fragile and are now being questioned. Is the current way of doing things serving our interests as well as we would like?

Big picture questions like sovereignty of supply chains, the growing divide between the 'haves and have-nots' that has proven to fuel community health concerns, and even the state of national health systems themselves. The opportunity for transformation is with us. A window in time when everything appears to be up for grabs. This is a time for envisioning the future we really want (described in Chapter 7, Element 1) and then following the elements identified within that chapter to nurture the space for adaptations to emerge.

For individuals, new choices about how and where to work and live may emerge. For businesses, this may be a time when entirely new business models are discovered. For the nation as a whole, it is possible that a new future emerges. There are many within the progressive political ranks calling for a rebuilding of the economy that is aligned with a more ecologically conscious and socially just future – a Green New Deal.

A new map to read the territory

I hope the connections between our new context and this book have been made and the relevance of the material within this book is clear. Most of all, I perceive this book as providing you with a new map with which to navigate the present and shape the future. If we use the old map, informed by Newtonian thinking (identified in Chapters 1 and 2), we will reinforce the very conditions that enabled the Coronavirus to emerge and pose such a threat. Employing a new map, the paradigm of complexity, is an adaptation in itself and I trust that this book provides you with the understanding of how to help yourself as a change agent to make that shift, in order to nurture the big shifts that we need for a better future – as assessed by us all, as we each make our contributions to it.

Josie McLean
Adelaide
April 2020

Contents

FIGURES

TABLES

CHAPTER 1

Why another book on change and leadership?

This book is for you if you are a change agent within an organisation and you want to be more confident and more effective at liberating changes that matter, in an ongoing manner. 'Change agent' includes those who are internal to the organisation and those who are external consultants or professional coaches working within the organisation. You may also be in a leadership position or role although I use the term exercising leadership as an action that a change agent undertakes in cultivating the environment for change.

The types of organisational challenges that you may be grappling with may include:

- innovating new ways of working in the post-pandemic crisis
- seeking more innovation – maybe delivering a digital transformation
- delivering more effective outcomes when working with complex challenges in the public service
- developing an organisation capable of being more adaptable.

In my experience, all of these outcomes are seen as a pathway to the most basic of all challenges: continued relevance and survival in a rapidly changing world.

Many change agents I speak with know that change is rarely as neat as the plan suggested it should be. Change is messy and difficult. As I talk with change agents, there are many stories about other people resisting change – but not us! Many change agents know that they have to bring people along on the journey but find it difficult in practice. Leading change can be stressful because our expectations of ourselves as change agents are not met by the delivery of the changes. It can become embarrassing to admit that often we don't know how to lead or manage change, despite having attended the courses and employed all the step-by-step tools.

Most importantly of all, these changes are also being considered within the context of very busy work lives. So many people tell me that they just don't have the head space or time to think about the required changes at all!

Understanding change differently

This book identifies and challenges the very assumptions that are generally made about change – what it is and how it occurs.

We can shift from understanding change as something that is decided at senior levels and communicated down the line, to understanding change as a process that we engage people in, enabling change to emerge all throughout the organisation.

Emergent change is the way experimentation, adaptation and change happen in nature or living systems. Emergent change is uncontrolled, but there is order and responsibility. It is not chaotic because it is aligned with an internal DNA which ensures that, for example, a tree remains a tree and does not spontaneously turn into a duck. An organisation's DNA is its lived vision, values and purpose – it has the capacity to generate order and cohesion.

Challenging the traditional view of change itself and how it happens opens the doors to adaptative change and ongoing business survival and relevance. As we all learn more about engaging with emergent change, we understand that the associated leadership is one characterised by engaging people in developing solutions. That engagement liberates creativity, develops personal strengths, encourages collaboration and opens the possibility of increased productivity to previously unimagined levels. The people involved will feel valued, satisfied and supported in their personal and professional development.

The outcomes that are possible with a shift in the way we perceive the world may sound like nirvana in comparison with most traditional hierarchical organisations. Such is the degree of waste that goes un-noticed within the traditional worldview of planned change models and processes.

The value to be unleashed – generating real change

Business survival and moving beyond to a flourishing, sustainable future means that every enterprise needs to have a greater capacity to learn, adapt and change.

As Figure 1 illustrates, there is an opportunity for a quantum leap in the quantity and meaningful quality of changes emerging as the paradigm informing the assumptions about what the organisation is and how it changes is aligned with the paradigm of complexity.

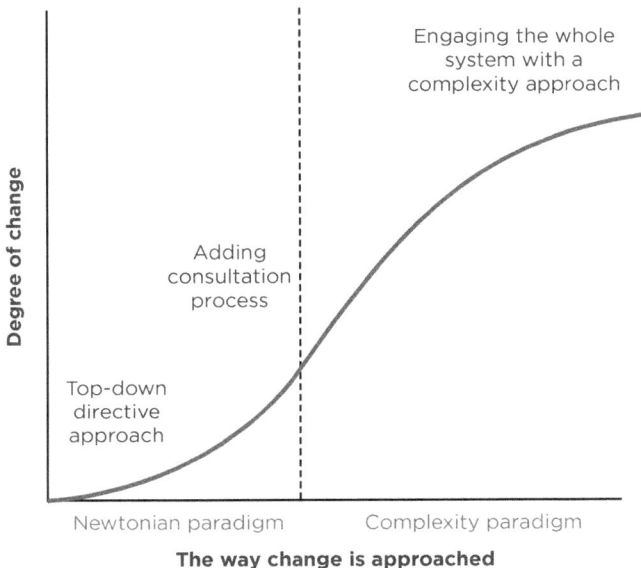

Figure 1: Degree of change increases with the paradigm shift

The typical top-down directive approach to change is a reflection of Newtonian paradigm assumptions that we will identify and investigate further. The engagement approach, on the other hand, is a consequence of perceiving the organisation as a living system or complex adaptive system. The area under the graph is the space that we are seeking to liberate. The paradigm shift that we will explore produces an exponential increase in the volume of change, and a significant qualitative adjustment in the human environment in which you and your people work.

Throughout this book I will use the terms **complexity** and **living systems** interchangeably. Complexity is a shorthand term for complex adaptive systems, which are mathematical models that intend to describe the behaviour of living systems. I prefer the term living systems. Humans are living systems, and because of this fact we already know something of how living systems function. We are more than objectified computer models. We each have our own complexity of experiences, personality and emotions that influence the complexity of the challenges we face and our responses. We are a part of the complexity.

Moving from understanding the world through the lens of the Newtonian paradigm to understanding complexity is a **paradigm shift**. Each of these paradigms can be viewed as almost the opposite of the other. It is a big shift in that sense. And in another sense, it is just a change in the lens through which we view the world. It's like wearing new glasses. It's a little shift in that sense – a little shift with big consequences. It's a **big little shift**.

Past paradigmatic shifts have enabled step changes

Humans have made such paradigm shifts before, from which great benefits have flowed. We have experienced paradigmatic shifts that have changed the way we view the world, and we also changed ourselves as a result.

For example, in 1539 Copernicus overturned a thousand years of doctrine that the sun revolves around the earth. In 1859, Charles Darwin published *On the Origin of Species*, touting natural selection as a process of evolution. This view was considered heresy because it challenged the accepted view of creationism. In 1865, Gregor Mendel showed that genetics were passed on from parent to child, not in an average fashion but over multiple generations with hybrid, dominant and recessive genes. And as recently as 1965, there was acceptance that plate tectonics is an explanation for large-scale geologic change. In 2000, a new term for a new geologic era was popularised by scientists: the Anthropocene.

We should take heart, therefore, that we are capable of transitioning through old paradigms and into new paradigms. Paradigms are, after all, just different ways we think about reality in our heads.

I believe we are capable of a lot more than just transitioning; I believe we are capable of discovering and liberating a great deal of lost human creativity and joy in the process. This is a transition that should be cherished and enjoyed because we have been so blissfully unaware of the costs of the old paradigm! Now, as we recognise these costs, we are able to evolve into reaping the rewards of human ingenuity in a different way – not merely technologically, but in the fullness of our human complexity. We will not leave technology behind, but rather integrate it as we transcend further into what it means to be humans collaborating in organisations.

This book identifies specific how to's

If the narrative I have offered about the need for a review of what change is and how it occurs is true, then some questions emerge.

1. What is the true nature and dynamic of change?

2. What do we need to do differently?

3. How might we do that differently?

4. How do we develop a culture of adaptability within our organisations?

I have been researching the answers to these four questions, theoretically and in practice, for 15 years. That research has included a doctorate in organisational transformation, complexity, leadership and sustainability. All these words come with loaded meaning, so just accept them at face value for now, but know that they will take on new meanings as we proceed through this book.

Human development

In the background of this 'how to' book is a field of study called human adult development as researched by people including Robert Kegan (1982), Suzanne Cook-Greuter and Jeffrey Soulen (2007), and Terri O'Fallon (2010). The study of human development can also be thought of as studying how humans make sense of our world and how we change the way we make sense of our reality over time. This is important because how we make sense of the world impacts what we perceive as being do-able or worth doing.

Increasing complexity is the evolutionary path of life – not only in regard to the biology of species and the natural ecologies of our planet, but also the ways in which we humans make sense of the world around us.

This book is not directly about adult development, but the research suggests that coming into contact with the ideas I present here may fuel your development and your capacity to liberate change in new ways. The paradigm of complexity is itself a way of making sense that is sometimes pointed to as being a specific stage of human development.

The complexity of human cognition has developed over time. You may recall the over-used quotation attributed to Einstein summarised as we can't solve our current problems with the same kind of thinking that created them. This idea captures, in a nutshell, why we need new ways of thinking about the challenges that we are confronted by. It also reflects the dynamic of how human cognitive capacity develops over time. The human brain adapts as it makes new sense of new realities.

This book and the topic will add to your range of perspectives and choices as you consider how to nurture change.

How to read and use this book

I am a practitioner, so I am interested in learning and sharing practices – I want you to be more confident and effective at leading change because our organisations and world surely need this capacity. To get to that point of applying the practices effectively, however, you need to appreciate the theory underpinning it – the **why** of what you are doing. We all operate from a theory, whether we are aware of it or not. To change our practices therefore requires us to **become aware of the theory** we want to consciously employ into the future.

The theory explores a new way of understanding how the world works that has been emerging since the 1950s. I know that you may be hankering to get to the doing, but what we do is a result of how we observe and interpret the world. So, I beg you to **slow down and read all the chapters** in the order that they are presented. This process takes you on an expedition of considering your organisation through the lens of living systems. Once we begin to understand that paradigm, we can get to the doing – exercising your leadership to generate the conditions for real change.

The Big Little Shift framework for your leadership

To develop your capacity to exercise leadership, you need skills, analytical frameworks and tools, and personal qualities and awareness, which all spring from an understanding and embodiment of the paradigm of living systems. These four layers of understanding how to cultivate adaptive change are summarised in Figure 2.

I have deliberately distilled the four layers because most books focus on the top two layers: skills and analytical frameworks and tools. They take the Newtonian paradigm for granted – not recognising the paradigm they are employing. The effectiveness of these two top layers is, however, very limited if the lower two layers are not considered. The way we perceive the world is fundamental to everything we do. And the way we perceive the world determines those qualities that will serve us best as we seek to change those things that matter to us.

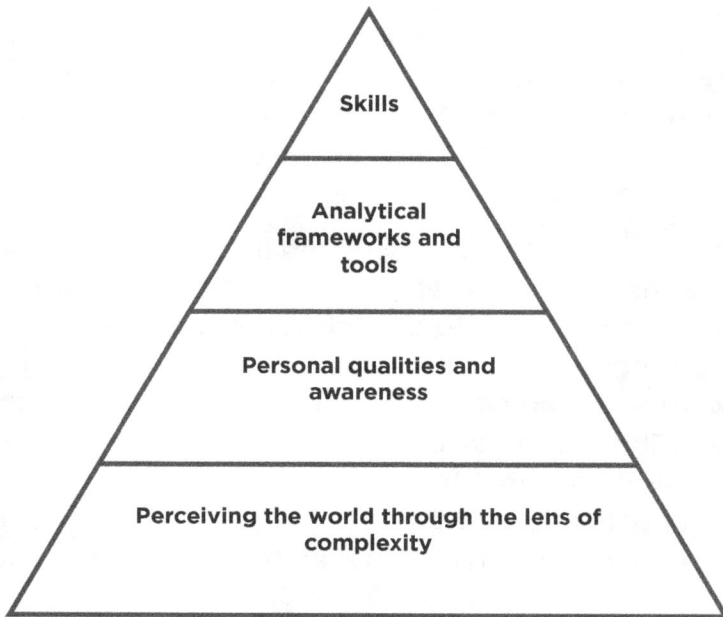

Figure 2: The Big Little Shift framework

The following chapters are ordered according to this model. Chapter 2 provides an **outline of the personal and organisational journey** that you might expect to experience as a change agent employing the Big Little Shift framework. Chapter 2 will also help you determine where you are in that journey now. From that basis, the four layers of the model will unfold from the bottom layer upwards, as described overleaf.

- Chapters 3–5 provide an in-depth view of understanding the world and our organisations when seen through the **lens of complexity**. We will identify and explore the assumptions that most organisations are unconsciously awash with from the Newtonian paradigm. In the process, we will identify new principles from which you might operate.

- Chapter 6 identifies the **personal qualities** that you might nurture within yourself as a result of employing the lens of complexity. The paradigm of complexity requires a more facilitative and nurturing leader – a **leader as a gardener** of people and the human environment. It is by nurturing, supporting, questioning, and encouraging diversity and curiosity that you will shape a team or organisation that is by its nature innovative, adaptable and flourishing. This is a distributed capacity for leadership that is self-organised.

- Chapters 7–9 identify the **seven elements of exercising your leadership** that take you on an arc from understanding the nature of your challenge, placing it within the context of the system of interest, and designing an experimental intervention in the system that engages others. This is the pragmatic doing that you may be hungry for.

- Chapter 10 identifies **specific skills and practices** that you might develop for yourself to hone your abilities to liberate emergent change.

- Finally, in the Chapter 11, I sum up our journey, making closing and important observations about the hope, simplicity and power inherent in employing a living systems or complexity lens.

Most chapters conclude with some questions for you to reflect upon. I encourage you to do this because these thinking exercises will aid your learning.

We will look at each layer of the model in Figure 2 separately, but of course they are not separate – they are part of a whole process that you will undertake. So, while they look separate in the model, as we discuss them we will find many interdependencies that make the exploration somewhat more circular rather than linear. The lines of separation may come to feel quite arbitrary. Nevertheless, the layers add specificity.

So, let's make a start by considering the whole journey we are about to embark upon and where you might be within that journey now.

Reflection questions

1. What challenges do you face in your team or organisation now?

   _____

   _____

   _____

   _____

   _____

   _____

2. How successfully have these challenges been addressed?

   _____

   _____

   _____

   _____

   _____

3. How are you being impacted by the context you have described in questions 1 and 2?

   _____

   _____

   _____

   _____

   _____

   _____

CHAPTER 2

What to expect when you hit the sweet spot

Before we move into the detail of this book, perhaps you would like a clearer idea of what to expect from implementing the practices that I recommend. The outcomes will be different for everyone of course, but the pathway will follow the patterns described below. You might like to track where you are on that pathway now and gain a sense of where you might move to next.

What might your journey look like?

In Table 1 I employ three different stages from **unaware** to **seeking** new ideas, and finally, to **mastery** at deliberately facilitating or influencing emergent change. The table is read from bottom to top and from left to right; creating a zig-zag path from number 1 to 9. Typically, we firstly focus on tools and skills which when integrated develop into rules or later, principles, that then become part of our way of being.

It is important to remember that change is emerging all the time – your aspiration therefore is to learn how to influence that emergence.

Table 1: Description of the journey to liberating adaptation

	Unaware	Seeking	Mastery
Being	Controlling (3)	Letting go of control (6)	Liberating adaptation (9)
Principles	Newtonian (2)	Edge of Newtonian (5)	Complexity (livings systems and Newtonian) (8)
Tools and skills	Communicating change (1)	Adding consultation (4)	Facilitator of emergent change (7)

Stage 1: Unaware

Over time you noticed that writing things into a plan does not often result in the implementation of the plan as written. So, you may have become interested in how to deliver the behavioural changes required to implement the plan. You may have become more interested in change and acquired the **tools, techniques and skills** of change management that we will explore in more detail in Chapter 3.

You learned and employed this more output-focused set of tools as best you could to **deliver a predetermined change**. These processes often looked more like project management briefs where changes were communicated or told to people, because senior management had decided that this is best for the whole organisation. It was a top-down process that you assumed was the only way of managing change. The assumptions you held, even if you were unaware of them, were the Newtonian assumptions that underpin control and command hierarchies.

Within the frame of control and command, a common outcome of imposed change is people feeling a bit like unengaged robots – just doing what they were told. Team members can feel undervalued and sceptical because they often feel unheard – their perspectives are not a part of the decision making. You didn't intend this outcome, and you didn't particularly like it.

It is the assumption that we can control outcomes within social and natural systems that makes the Newtonian paradigm self-limiting in the sphere of change and adaptation.

Stage 2: Seeking

Over time, you became aware that something else is needed. You felt a desire to have people feeling happier about being involved in change. You discovered that it may be possible to acquire some new tools and techniques that **make people feel as though they have ownership**. This felt like progress, and it was. You now have a mixture of some change management techniques and some consultative techniques. The change itself was still predominately top-down and predetermined – but it generated some better outcomes.

You achieved more involvement and a growing sense of goodwill. You were working at the edge of the Newtonian paradigm, and maybe you started to notice and become more aware of the tacit assumptions underpinning your choices.

You gradually experimented – and started to let go of your need for control. You noticed that when you held a sense of knowing the right answer more lightly, more possibilities emerged, and people were more engaged and alive. You may have noticed that some team members took more encouragement to become more involved. They had learned not to be involved, and some even enjoyed pointing the finger at those in authority. But, over time, change started to become interesting and more participative. It also became a bit messier and less predictable, but despite this, more change seemed to be occurring.

Stage 3: Mastery

One day you entered a room and had an amazing conversation with a group of people at work about change.

It may have been a conversation for which you had prepared yourself and them very well. The conversation may have employed a predetermined facilitative process to enable the emergence from the group that represented the whole system. Or, it may be that the conversation was impromptu.

Either way, the conversation was within a lightly structured environment, and it was about things that people cared about – central to the key concerns of the organisation at the time. Everyone was focused on the vision, values and purpose of the organisation – and how to achieve that vision more fully. Keen awareness of these three important reference points enabled everyone to participate in the conversation about what changes were needed. The focus on these reference points was a reflection of your growing understanding of how living systems behave and naturally, spontaneously adapt when needed.

The conversation was facilitated skilfully, with a subtle and deft touch that gently encouraged people to inquire right down to the assumptions from which the structure of the existing reality emerged. People were forthright, and a few home truths were exposed. Vulnerability and trust grew together. You, like others, left the conversation feeling alive and activated – ready to do what was required. Maybe what was required was another conversation – everyone was willing to do that. You realised that you had just facilitated the **liberation of new possibilities – adaptation**.

You were all nurturing a way of working, a culture, that had the capacity of being adaptive.

You notice that you were personally very aware of the two paradigms – Newtonian and complexity – and you knew when to appropriately apply each.

Your development

The three stages in Table 1 represent the journey that you are already on. This book attempts to provide you with a guide to your own development as a catalyst of emergent, adaptive change. An adaptive change that is able not only to respond to changes in the environment around it, but also to contribute towards shaping that environment with a vision. A vision that will mingle with a multitude of other peoples' visions before the emergent outcome manifests in the wider world.

If you are successful, there is a bigger game to be played. The game of whole systems redesigns that are organisational, industry, or society wide. Maybe you are already actively involved at these larger levels too?

What might your organisation look like?

Table 2 provides a snapshot of the paradigmatic shift we are about to investigate together. When the shift to perceiving the organisation as a living or complex adaptive system has been embraced by the organisation as a whole, employees will be engaged in adaptation in an ongoing manner.

Team members will be brought alive afresh as they pick up their responsibility within the system and are valued as active participants. The creativity that is required at the heart of innovation will be exuding from people who work to their natural strengths (a force of nature in its own right). New teams will spontaneously appear as your people gather the people they need to bring together to resolve complex issues. Their interpersonal skills will need to be developed, and they will also improve from participation in the discussions that you lead. Decisions will be made by those closest to the issue and with reference to those impacted. Decisions will be responsible because of the way in which a systemic view is always taken, and others are involved.

Adaptive leadership will be exercised by anyone and everyone as is appropriate. You will have nurtured a system-wide capacity. This is **distributed leadership** – not just because it is spread across many individuals but also because they are all energised by a common DNA – your organisational vision, purpose and values.

Your organisation will have placed the capacity to adapt at the very heart of its culture and discovered the powerful force of self-organisation.

Words such as **nimble**, **agile** and **adaptive** will be lived, nurturing a powerful, positive human environment within which essential changes, including technological, can be delivered with maximum benefit to all. Benefits will flow to your team members, the organisation, your customers and society at large.

Table 2: Contrast between organisations viewed through the lenses of Newtonian and complexity paradigms

Newtonian: Predetermined change process	Complexity: Emergent change process
Perceiving change as an object that can be identified and predetermined by senior management.	Perceiving change as an ever-present potential waiting to be liberated.
Episodic change.	Evolving and continuous adaptive change.
Plans are communicated to those who need to know.	Changes emerge with reference to organisational identity (vision, purpose and values) Broad participation encouraged around a central question – self-organisation emerges.
Most people feel undervalued. The process of telling means many people do not make sense of the need for change.	People are involved and are valued. Their strengths and interests are nurtured – they grow and develop. The process of determining what to do enables adaptive work within each person.
Success measured in terms such as 'on time and on budget' – neat and tidy.	Success is indicated by the degree of engagement and the way the change is embedded into daily habits at work.

Reflection questions

1. As you read through the three stages in Table 1, which
    stage represents your current centre of gravity?

    _____

    _____

    _____

    _____

    _____

    _____

2. Reflecting on the organisational journey, which paradigm
    is your organisation predominantly operating from?
    (It may be that both paradigms are present. Which
    predominates where and when?)

    _____

    _____

    _____

    _____

    _____

    _____

CHAPTER 3

Understanding change

Learning and change

I have already been using the term change a great deal. Let's spend a moment reflecting on what I mean by the words **change**, **adaptation**, and **transformation**. These are terms that are bandied about and used interchangeably in popular media; however, they are different types or degrees of change.

Learning and change are not the same, but they are connected. When we genuinely learn something, it changes or alters what we do. There is action attached to real learning. If you say you know something but you don't act upon it – then I'm sorry, you don't really understand it. This distinguishes learning from education that is technical and resides in your memory yet is not acted upon.

Learning is the precursor to **change.**

Chris Argyris and Donald Schön (1978) introduced the world to the notions of single- and double-loop learning, as they explored what Argyris sometimes referred to as human beings' **skilful non-learning**. As they explored non-learning, which you must agree still seems prevalent in today's contemporary organisations, they developed the notions of single- and double-loop learning. These distinctions are represented pictorially in Figure 3, with the added idea of triple- loop learning that Argyris identified as a learner questioning their context and purpose. Figure 3 clarifies the way in which I am employing the terms change, adaptation and transformation that I explain in the following section.

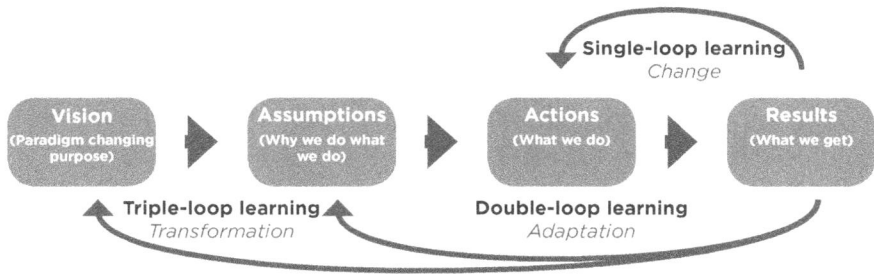

Figure 3: Single-, double- and triple-loop learning illustrated

Single- and double-loop learning

Single-loop learning occurs when there is a discrepancy between the desired result and actual result, prompting a person to take a different action, but without challenging the underlying values or beliefs that influence that action. The person **changes** the work done but little else.

Single-loop learning is the predominant form of change within organisations and our society at present. It is the easiest because it doesn't challenge personal and often unconscious values and beliefs that determine what we do. This type of change includes efficiency gains and most continuous improvement processes. We have milked this type of change for a long time, and it has served us well in many ways – but although it is a necessary type of change, it is no longer sufficient to meet the needs of adaptation today, let alone those of the decades yet to come.

An often-overlooked feature of single-loop learning that Argyris (2003) highlighted from his years of working within organisations is that single-loop learning is primarily defensive in nature. He attributed it to the source of why organisational change initiatives are so tricky and ineffective. Single-loop learning, says Argyris, is also associated with a lack of self-awareness.(Argris 2003, p3) These ideas connect to those of Heifetz, Grashow & Linsky, who identify **technical** challenges – ones where we think we already know the answers (2009). We will explore technical challenges in depth in Chapter 7.

Double-loop learning occurs when the discrepancy between the desired and the actual result prompts those involved to stop and question the underlying values and beliefs – or assumptions – that influence how the problem itself is perceived. This process is **adaptive** work, as described by Heifetz, Grashow & Linsky (2009). This type of change is complex and messy because human emotions associated with values and beliefs are now involved. As a change agent, becoming competent at leading this type of change is now a necessity.

Double-loop learning and adaptive work are the processes of **learning about learning**. These processes develop self-awareness and awareness of others. My experience is that they also develop systems awareness or intelligence.

To use a common metaphor, simple (single-loop) change occurs as people shift the deck chairs on the *Titanic* as it sinks. Adaptive (double-loop) change occurs when the captain of the *Titanic* challenges the belief that the *Titanic* will never sink and alters the course in time to avoid the iceberg.

Triple-loop learning and transformation

Triple-loop learning occurs with a shift in context or the collective **vision** and represents a paradigm shift in the learning – where not one set of values and beliefs is challenged, but an entire framework of them.

A **paradigm** is a framework of ideas that enable the exploration of a particular sphere of research and practice. This framework allows people to understand and predict what may occur when specific actions are taken (even if the prediction is that it is uncertain, and we don't know what will happen). A paradigm is like a giant model of theory and practice.

A paradigm shift opens the possibility of an entirely new way of perceiving and taking action because it completely reframes the challenge. Triple-loop learning and **transformation** in a business context is associated with the emergence of an entirely **new organisational identity**: a transformed purpose, vision, and set of values. One example of this type of shift may be a coal mining business shifting the view of their business from mining to energy supply. That would be a complete reframe.

Adaptation is a term that comes from the study of the paradigm of complexity or living systems. However, adaptation can be viewed as reactive in nature – reacting to changes within the environment around you. Humans have consciousness or awareness that can be folded back onto itself. We can go beyond merely reacting; we can consciously and proactively shape and redesign the broader system itself.

One of my favourite systems thinkers, Donella Meadows, directs our thinking to more than reactive change – to redesigning entire systems:

> *Systems can't be controlled, but they can be designed and redesigned. We can't surge forward with certainty into a world of no surprises, but we can expect surprises and learn from them and even profit from them. We can't impose our will upon a system. We can listen to what the system tells us, and discover how its properties and our values can work together to bring forth something much better than could ever be produced by our will alone.*

(Meadows 2008, pp. 169–170)

As an example, Interface Carpets, a carpet manufacturing business, disrupted its business model to shift from manufacturing more and more carpet to manufacturing, renting, and recycling its carpets. It is now more of a service company, renting the use of flooring rather than manufacturing and selling carpet in the traditional sense. That's a paradigm shift or a triple-loop transformational change that also impacts the broader industry or system.

What then, does 'change management' mean?

Given these three different ways of understanding learning and change, what does the term **change management** mean?

I began my early working life, over 30 years ago, as a financial analyst in the newly emerging activity of corporate strategic planning. I often tell people about how lovely my plans were! They were strong on analysis of the market, economic trends, demographics and predictive forecasts. They were developed with direction from and consultation with the board and the executive team. However, I had one defining experience, soon after releasing the latest plan. As I entered the branch office to speak with the branch manager, he stood and zeroed in on direct eye contact with me. He lifted the plan that was on his desk so I could see him and the plan. He then very slowly and deliberately opened the top drawer on his desk and dropped the plan into it. With his eyes fixed on mine, he firmly slammed the drawer shut. The words were not spoken, but the message was clear: 'I'm not happy! Your plan is crap!' From that moment, I became very interested in the intersection of strategy development, people, process, change and implementation.

One reason that my plan suffered 30 years ago was that I assumed that if people were told what to do, they would do it. At that time, we were not even thinking about change management. Australian practice was somewhat behind that overseas where in the 1960s the idea of change management had begun to appear. During the 1980s, when restructuring was popular in Australia, change management was recognised and we began to tussle with the problem of implementing change **smoothly**, **efficiently** and **effectively**. Who doesn't want that?

John P. Kotter's 'Eight-step process to lead change' emerged as an article in 1995 in response to his research into 100 large businesses trying to reinvent themselves to serve changing markets. His observation was that *'a few of these corporate change efforts have been very successful. A few have been utter failures. Most fall somewhere in between, with a distinct tilt toward the lower end of the scale'* (cited from the reprint Kotter 2007, p. 96). A number of other similarly inspired models, such as the Change Management Model and, more recently, Awareness–Desire–Knowledge–Ability–Reinforcement (ADKAR), have been actively promoted by the consulting profession and eagerly grasped by managers.

The desire for the ability to change is strong because if a business cannot change, it cannot survive for long in today's rapidly changing world. But despite the adoption of linear step-by-step change management processes and practices, the research continues to indicate that at least 70% (and up to 90%) of all organisational change initiatives fail to deliver their intended outcomes (Beer & Nohria 2000; Higgs & Rowland 2005). These results continue to emerge. For example, Doblin (a Deloitte business) in a study entitled *Beacons for business model innovations*, examined the success of more than 5,000 business model innovations. They reported that only 4.5% of innovations have been successful over a 15-year period (Tuff & Wunker 2014). Regardless of the specific statistic, change continues to be difficult, and perhaps that should not be a revelation given our recent identification of three different types of learning: single-, double- and triple-loop.

Why is change management so difficult within our organisations?

The change management process and models are all slightly different, with varying emphasis on technological infrastructure, human emotions and behaviours, and systems and processes. But if examined, they exhibit most or all of the following key characteristics:

- Predominantly top-down direction to change, whether from the CEO's office or the team leader's.

- Predetermined outcomes and a generally short timeline with a project management flavour.

- An assumption that people will resist the change and that rational persuasion or good communication (sometimes labelled 'consultation') will get the change over the line.

- A bottom-line assumption that 'if you can't change the people, then you will need to change the people!' – alternative views are not very well tolerated.

As the change is planned, it is assumed that it will be simple, easy and quick – despite most change practitioners' evidence to the contrary. Change management is underpinned by unconscious Newtonian assumptions. Most change management processes and tools assume a single-loop learning process by default.

Many of the managers that I speak with either feel inadequate to lead change well or they feel stressed and incompetent because it's not working out the way it was planned.

The reason for the discomfort and stress is that **we have not correctly understood what change is or how it occurs**. That is not any manager's fault. Most are just acting on what they have been taught either at university in their MBA or culturally by watching other managers and intuiting the expectations.

Since the 1950s a new way of understanding how the world operates has emerged with the scientific study of natural systems such as rainforests and weather patterns. This new understanding has shone a light on what we had previously not even noticed. Unconscious assumptions about how the world operates are so deeply socialised within each of us and our organisations that we have not even thought to question them. We have been swimming like fish in water and completely unaware of the water. That water has been and is the Newtonian paradigm.

The deeply socialised Newtonian paradigm

For the last 300 years, Western society has been under the powerful yet unconscious influence of the Newtonian paradigm, also referred to as the scientific paradigm. It bears the name of the person who was the major force behind the development of the paradigm, Sir Isaac Newton. In its time, the Newtonian paradigm was revolutionary, born of the Enlightenment, which promoted the application of rational rather than mythic logic.

Newton perceived the universe as a clock. Earth was one part of that clock. The paradigm's promise is that if we can just understand enough about the behaviour of the clock and each of its parts, then we will be able to predict and, by inference, control all the workings. An assumption of this paradigm is that all the workings and the behaviour of the clock are discoverable and knowable.

The Newtonian paradigm assumes that:

- there are discoverable rules or laws that govern behaviour
- direct and linear cause and effect exists (i.e. the size of the outcome directly correlates to the size of the input)
- consistent and replicable results are possible (i.e. if you do the same thing more than once, you obtain the same outcome)
- predictability and certainty are the norm (resulting from the above characteristics)
- problems may be solved by reducing the problem to its parts and resolving the issue at that level (reductionism).

The Newtonian paradigm encouraged the innate human desire for certainty and security and led to a belief that we can predetermine and predict outcomes and the paths to achieving those outcomes. This belief lives on within organisations today, most subtly, yet powerfully, in the form of unconscious assumptions underpinning the majority of organisational cultures. These unconscious assumptions and beliefs about 'how we do things around here' are values that have stood the test of time (Schein 1990).

As examples, the beliefs that underpin the Newtonian paradigm encourage organisations to create strategic planning and functional silos, cascade goals and key performance indicators

(KPIs) to different departments and individuals ('management by objectives'), and predetermine values before 'rolling them out' over the organisation in an effort to regulate behaviours.

Your actions are influenced by Newtonian assumptions

Importantly for our current inquiry into what change is, the Newtonian paradigm understands change as something that is done to the clock or machine by an external agent. Newton believed that the agent who maintained the universal clock was God – the key authority. And here lies an interesting link to leadership and change within our organisations today.

Remember the key characteristics of change management identified earlier? The characteristics were predominately top-down predetermined outcomes delivered in an authoritarian style. The similarity is striking and no coincidence.

It is the Newtonian paradigm influencing us all through deeply held and unconscious beliefs, impacting our actions and the results we achieve. Senior management – the key authorities – determine what needs to change, a plan is developed and actioned with the expectation that people will do what is necessary to implement it, and the change will be delivered on time and on budget. We keep doing this over and over in a single-loop learning cycle. It's time to apply double-loop learning and question the assumptions we are making.

Also, note the separation between identifying the intended future state and implementation. It is this separation that is the root cause of the difficulty with implementation.

We have applied the Newtonian paradigm inappropriately to natural and social systems that we now understand might be better served by employing a different paradigm – the paradigm of living systems, or the paradigm of complexity.

Like models, all paradigms are wrong, yet helpful

All paradigms are human constructions – they are not real in the sense that you can find one in nature and touch it. Like the famous mathematician George Box (1979), I subscribe to the view that all models are wrong, because they are abstractions of the real world, but some are useful.

Paradigms are also approximations of the real world. To say that an organisation is a machine is not true, and yet this story, with its Newtonian underpinning, has existed for a long time. You might reflect for a moment on phrases that are commonly used to describe organisations:

- 'Functioning like a well-oiled machine.'
- 'Resources are coming together like well-functioning cogs.'
- 'Operating with machine-like consistency and efficiency.'

To say that an organisation is a living system is also not true because unlike humans, it has no equivalent to our skin that forms a boundary between us and the external environment.

To say that we might understand more about how an organisation operates and therefore how we might enable it to operate more effectively by viewing it as a living system can, in my experience, be very helpful.

The paradigm of complexity – the epicentre of the big little shift

A living system reproduces itself from its component elements. For example, you are a living system – your body repairs itself from its constituent parts by regenerating new cells from existing DNA code. A tree is a living system because it reproduces itself from its DNA and existing energy and materials available within it. Rather than being inanimate objects without intelligence, all living systems are understood to have some degree of cognition or intelligence. That intelligence is not identical to human consciousness, but it enables living systems to adapt to information about changing circumstances or environments. (If you would like to understand more about this intelligence, I recommend reading Maturana, Varela and Uribe's theory of autopoiesis (1974).)

It is the flow of information throughout living systems that creates the interdependence between the parts – from your smallest cells to the Amazonian forests to civilisations. Learning to appreciate the world through the lens of complexity is a step into trying to perceive and understand wholeness in all the senses of the word: wholeness in regard to the complexity of each living system, its history and its potential, or, to paraphrase, a whole world in which every whole human, plant and animal is a part of each other's environment (Bateson 1972). In this book, I am aware that I am but scratching the surface of humanity's existing awareness of complexity. This scratching, however, should be enough to assist and guide you on your journey, as it has me.

Living systems behave in ways that are almost the exact opposite of the ways we might expect them to behave if we applied the Newtonian paradigm. This means that what we have previously accepted as normal or common sense is due for a ground-shaking shift.

Living systems are:

- self-replicating and self-regulating from their constituent elements (that is what makes them living)

- sensitive to initial starting conditions – small variations make big differences over time

- coupled or connected to the larger system in which they exist, which means they are interdependent through the flow of information

- influenced by indirect and non-linear cause and effect (often referred to as the 'butterfly effect' originating from Edward Lorenz (Hilborn, 2003) who used the example of a flapping wings on one side of the world, creating a tornado on the other side of the world.)

- inherently unpredictable and inconsistent in their behaviour

- self-organising with reference to their identity.

Most importantly, we are not able to control living systems, but because we live within them, we can influence the powerful natural forces that are at play – liberating new possibilities from within them. We are not powerless. In fact, we might be more powerful. We might have more influence than when we use our own will to pursue plans to deliver Newtonian-inspired predetermined and controlled outcomes.

If the Newtonian paradigm is fundamentally about *controlling* what will be, then the living system paradigm is fundamentally about *liberating* what might be.

How does adaptation occur?

If we focus our attention on when and how adaptation occurs within living systems, we are struck by the following facts.

- Learning, experimentation and the emergence of adaptation occurs spontaneously and without a blueprint developed by any authority figure. No one is in charge. Change is emergent rather than planned.

- There is broad participation of all agents within the system as they make sense of new information coming in from the external environment or from novel responses internally.

- An adaptation occurs with reference to the living system's identity, which, in the case of an organisation, can be thought of as its lived (rather than espoused) vision, purpose and values.

- Change is experimental in its nature. No one knows if it will be successful. The organism tries something out. Nature is full of experiments – some fail and some work out well in the sense that the living system flourishes.

The ability to learn and adapt is a life force. If an entity is dead, it no longer possesses the ability to adapt or change. Figure 4 summarises these ideas pictorially.

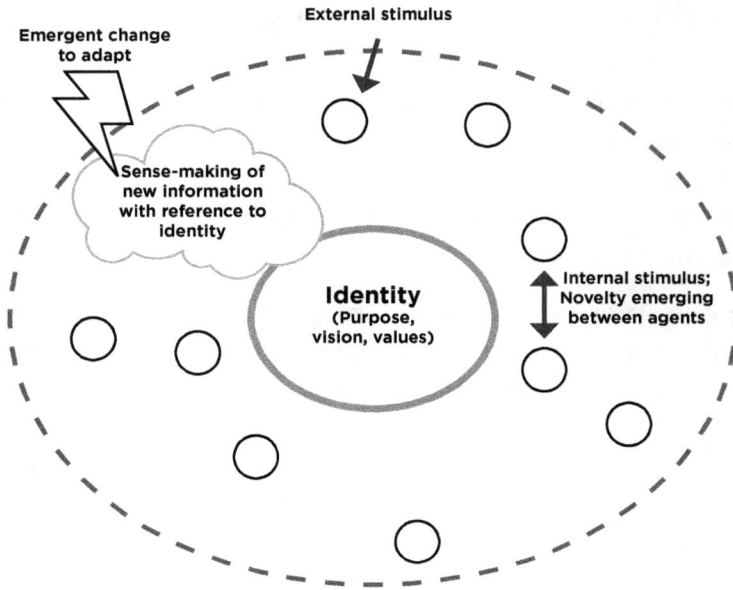

Figure 4: Adaptation emerges from a stimulus (adapted from McLean 2017, p52)

The absence of an authority figure and a blueprint can initially be alarming for some executives and managers who, being more familiar with the control embedded in existing hierarchical organisations, believe that a lack of authority is a recipe for chaos. However, it is not chaos. Order exists but in a different form, because living systems also have the quality of self-organisation. Cohesion is inherent in the system by virtue of the living system's identity – which in a human body is DNA and in an organisation is its **lived vision, purpose and values**.

This means that organisational **adaptation emerges**, like personal adaptation, as people make sense of new information with reference to their purpose and important values. We will return to this point, because it links directly to organisational culture and how to exercise your leadership.

In the next chapter I will identify the key principles to guide your leadership derived from examining the underlying behaviour of living systems or complexity.

Reflection questions

1. How often are single-loop learning and double-loop learning strategies employed within your team?

    _____

    _____

2. What has been a recent example of double-loop learning at work? What happened as people engaged with this type of learning? How easy was it to manage?

    _____

    _____

3. Review the list of assumptions about how the Newtonian paradigm behaves and make a list of activities you undertake at work that reflect this paradigm.

    _____

    _____

4. How well does the living systems view of change or adaptation emerging from the system align with your experience of change?

    _____

    _____

5. How does your need and desire for control show up at work and at home?

    _____

    _____

CHAPTER 4

Key leadership principles within complexity

Introduction

The behaviour of living systems implies certain principles to help us understand how we can cultivate the conditions for learning and adaptation within the system. These principles can guide you as you exercise your leadership for change.

You will observe these principals also coming to life and underpinning the frameworks and tools in Chapters 7–10, where we inquire into what, specifically, to do. Being aware of these principles will help you choose what to do when and why – and seed your transformational journey.

I use the word **transformational** very deliberately because your purpose should alter as a result – this is triple-loop learning. The broader perspective will eventually shift your purpose from a specific goal to **nurturing the health of the whole system.**

Shifting your purpose from single-goal outcomes

I shared the following story recently on a Facebook page and a member commented that this story may have happened in 1950, but it wouldn't happen today. Really? I see reductionist approaches everywhere – every day. You might too if you start looking for them. Reductionism is the opposite of a living systems approach and is the most common way we tend to respond to challenges.

In the early 1950s, the Dayak people in Borneo suffered from malaria. The World Health Organization had a solution: they sprayed large amounts of DDT to kill the mosquitoes that carried the malaria. The mosquitoes died, the malaria declined; so far, so good. But there were side-effects.

Among the first was that the roofs of people's houses began to fall down on their heads. It seemed that the DDT was killing a parasitic wasp that had previously controlled thatch-eating caterpillars. Worse, the DDT- poisoned insects were eaten by geckoes, which were eaten by cats. The cats died, the rats flourished, and people were threatened by out-breaks of sylvatic plague and typhus.

To cope with these problems, which it had itself created, the World Health Organization was obliged to parachute 14,000 live cats into Borneo.

(Lovins & Lovins 1995 cited in Wahl 2017)

This is a cautionary tale about a reductionist approach that sees just one problem and has a focus on achieving one goal. That tunnel vision often creates '**unintended side-effects'**. These are not side-effects though. From a living systems perspective they are non-linear cause and effect in action – effects emerging due to interdependence between different parts of the system, over a longer time frame and broader geographical spread than initially anticipated.

Keep your attention and intention on the health of the whole.

Principles with application at many levels

As we discuss living systems and think predominately about organisational change, it's important to remember that the principles we explore are applicable at different scales – from organisations, to teams and to individuals. This generalisation is possible because living systems can be described being organised as a **holarchy** rather than hierarchy (Koestler 1976).

A **holon** is a whole and complete part of a larger system. That is, living systems are organised as a series of nested subsystems within larger systems, as illustrated in Figure 5. Here we see an organisational holarchy with an individual, whole and complete, within a team, whole and complete, within an organisation, within a community, within the natural environment. Each holon is whole and complete and a part of other holons.

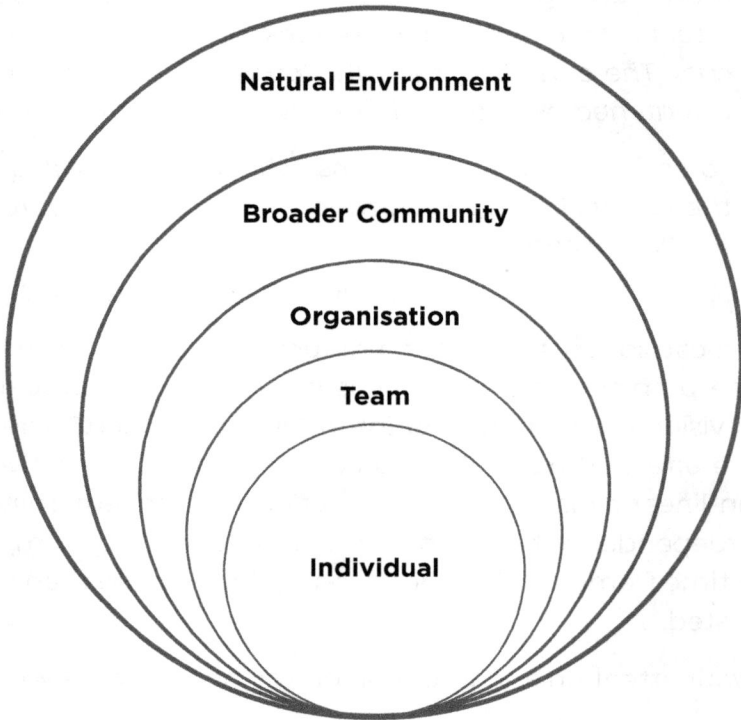

Figure 5: Illustration of organisational holarchy

Figure 5 shows all holons joining at the bottom in a way that attempts to illustrate this interdependence and being a part of each other's environment. All holons are in continuous relationship with each other – all interdependent all of the time. The principles shared here work for all holons – all being whole and complete living system within themselves.

Table 3 identifies relevant principles from the paradigm of living systems and derives leadership principles and behaviours to guide you. They are not shown in any specific order, because each is as important as the others. Each is connected to all others, and you will notice the overlap between them as I provide a narrative for each principle.

Table 3: Leadership principles and behaviours derived from the paradigm of living systems (adapted from McLean 2017, p. 88)

Principles of living systems and emergent change	Leadership principles and behaviours
1. Adaptation is a constant potential of a living system.	• Meaning-making conversations are the change. • Engage people in conversations that are not limited by predetermined outcomes – be curious and seek to learn and adapt together. • Ask questions that help people make new systemic meaning. • Hold the space for conversations that challenge existing mental models and long-held values. • Liberate the best from people by facilitating their self-actualisation and allowing them to work from their strengths and passion – liberate intrinsic motivation. • Be mindful of the influence of processes or systems to either reinforce or decrease the influence of feedback loops.

2. The system is irreducibly uncertain and unpredictable.	• Give up desire for control – seek the more powerful option to influence and liberate possibilities with consideration given to the systemic nature of any given situation. • Starting conditions are important – carefully consider who should be present at initial conversations. • Experiment to see what may work – embrace 'error' as a basis for learning. • Specific measurements may not be suitable, due to the way in which measures tend to focus on one part of the system – develop an understanding of indicators within the system. • Articulate your own vision of the change process and associated values to monitor the emergence of the process.
3. Identity is referenced in meaning-making.	• Create an emergent and shared vision of what people really want, and employ the embedded shared values. • Those exercising leadership will influence more effectively if they embody the values and live the vision – reinforcing the identity of the system.

4. Self-organisation emerges with broad participation.	• Locate responsibility with people and allow them to self-organise – do not impose control or organisation. Allow self-organisation to emerge. • Be inclusive and invite broad participation – appreciate the perspectives offered in groups. • Treat information as the lifeblood of the organisation – keep it circulating and accessible as widely as possible. Enable transparency.
5. Novelty within the system may be a source of adaptation.	• Appreciate and work with genuine diversity and 'hold the space' for these differences to amplify into new solutions.

Principle 1: Adaptation is a constant potential of a living system

In Chapter 3 we discussed how adaptation emerges, enabling living systems to adapt to external stimulus or internal novelty (Figure 4). There are three important elements that I'd like to discuss which are associated with liberating adaptation from within people:

- mental models
- intrinsic motivation
- the influence of the larger system.

Change is fundamentally about authoring a new story for us individually and collectively. Some of these are stories that you have been telling yourself about yourself for a very long time – since childhood. Some are patterns that exist in our nervous systems. Some show up in our daily interactions as triggers that may see us behave in seemingly irrational ways. Others are long-held loyalties and connections to other people that exist within each of us as mental models and elements of our lives that we cherish – our values.

Understanding and identifying mental models

The concept of mental models was popularised by Peter Senge in his famous book *The Fifth Discipline*, where he explained them as:

> *deeply ingrained assumptions, generalizations or even pictures or images that influence how we understand the world and how we take action. Very often, we are not consciously aware of our mental models or the effects they have on our behaviour.*   (Senge 1994, p 8)

We all have many, many mental models. They are deeply socialised in our families, our organisations and the societies in which we live. They show up in businesses in regard to strategies that are developed and the way products and services are marketed. A classic example is that of Swiss watchmakers who believed that digital watches would never become appealing to a mass market.

Mental models are neither right nor wrong. They are usually a generalisation from a specific experience where the individual learned this belief. The question is whether the specific mental model is serving you, or us, well. Will it continue to serve us well into the future? If not, we are at liberty to choose another mental model. With awareness, we can choose to have our thinking rather than our thinking having us!

Making new meaning – connecting mental models and values

Mental models are also closely related to the idea of values. The *Oxford English Dictionary* defines values as '*principles or standards of behaviour; one's judgement of what is important in life*' and cites an example of a source as '*they internalize their parents' rules and values*'. Those rules could easily be argued to be mental models. Similarly, if mental models are deeply held beliefs, so are values. We value those beliefs. (Heifetz, in his adaptive leadership framework, which we will employ in Chapter 7, identifies adaptive work as a reprioritisation of values (Heifetz, Grashow & Linsky 2009).)

An element of your role as you cultivate the conditions for adaptation, is to help reveal or bring into the light of day from the hidden recesses of unconscious minds the mental models and values that are influencing the current choices and decisions. Once these mental models and values are revealed, your job is to guide those people to assess for themselves whether they need to adopt different mental models/values in order to survive and thrive into the future.

It is easiest to do this by listening deeply for the mental models and asking powerful questions (a skill that I will say more about in Chapter 10). Research from neuroscience indicates that people need to have their own 'ah-ha' moments for new neural pathways to be created to think in new ways (Schwartz & Rock 2006).

Your leadership task is to develop conversational processes that are focused on amending or changing meaning-making. Meaning comes from understanding the context and relevance of the issue. Therefore, to cultivate the conditions for adaptation, we need to provide places where people can understand the challenge within their context – from within their own stories – in a way that is relevant to them (Bateson 2002).

Creativity through engaging with self-actualisation

An often-overlooked sphere of creativity and innovation is associated with which motivations serve it best. Three areas of research that are relevant and important – self-actualisation, strengths, and interest or passion – are described below.

1. Maslow (1959) ignited thinking about self-actualisation and argued that the movement towards self-actualisation is a fundamental and inherent tendency within humans. It could be said, within our context of living systems, that self-actualisation is a natural force of nature; people naturally

want to become more and more of who they were born to be. An outcome of being engaged with the process of self-actualisation is that people are more comfortable in their own skin and more willing to take risks. They will explore new ideas with a sense of adventure to see what will work. These are qualities that are fundamental to being more innovative.

2. Research into personal strengths from positive psychology undertaken by the Gallup Organisation indicates that people are more creative in their problem-solving when working in ways that engage their personal strengths (Buckingham & Clifton 2001). Working to personal strengths is also one pathway to self-actualisation.

3. Another area of research shows that people are more creative when working in areas that they are interested in and even passionate about (Amabile 1997; Amabile, Hadley & Kramer 2002; Maslow 1959). Amabile has explored further to suggest a link between creativity and interest (or passion) for a topic. And the positive correlation between empowering leadership styles and creativity has also been demonstrated.

The leadership implication for adaptive and transformational change is to enable people to work from and with their intrinsic motivations as much as possible. This suggests that invitations to work on adaptive challenges should be voluntary – results will be less than optimal if you force people to participate. Understanding their interests and motivations is important.

From a living systems perspective, this principle is an example of **working with the powerful natural forces** that exist within each of us human beings – powerful natural forces that exist within all living systems.

Maintaining a systemic awareness

As you seek to cultivate the conditions for adaptation, you need also to be aware of how the larger system is influencing people. For example, working as a team is fundamentally a way of collaborating. And collaborating means sharing ideas and performing together with a high degree of mutual rather than solely individual accountability. When a team member chooses to operate within a true team, they are, in an unspoken manner, handing over their next performance review outcome to the rest of their team. Unless the organisation has shifted from individual performance reviews to collective team reviews, the knowledge of that inconsistency exists in people's minds and influences their choices about committing to the team fully – or not.

Your awareness also needs to be on the other people and processes that are exerting an invisible yet substantial influence on those with whom you are working. We will identify tools and frameworks to help analyse such situations in Chapter 7.

Principle 2: The system is irreducibly uncertain and unpredictable

Living systems are inherently unpredictable. Some participants, particularly those with hard science backgrounds, ignite fiery discussion around this point in my workshops. But it is a feature of living systems that the feedback loops of interdependence make the systems inherently unpredictable. This means that the goals we often set and try to achieve within organisations are often unhelpful constructs when operating in complex situations – particularly over longer time frames and broader geographical distances. I know that may sound like heresy, but there it is. We will explore this facet of complexity in more depth in Chapter 9 when we discuss how to monitor the progress of your adaptation initiative.

The essential point to take away here is **you can't know the answer** – any answer that relates to a natural and or social system. And this means that you and your people must learn your way forward. There are two facets to this learning.

The first relates back to the discussion around mental models and neuroscience. Each person must have their 'ah-ha' moment. You will find it difficult to tell them this. So even if you think you know the answer, people must still 'ah-ha' for themselves.

Secondly, through the lens of complexity, the system is so complex that it requires **more than one perspective** to enable effective new ways forward to emerge. As a leader, you only have your perspective. You must engage other perspectives for the best possible understanding (at this time) to emerge. Another way of understanding this idea is that the complexity of the solution needs to meet the complexity of the challenge. Your single perspective does not provide enough complexity. So, the way forward is learning together.

Also, at the beginning of specific initiatives, pay attention to who is present and on-board, or not, because small variations in starting conditions can influence the unfolding of the initiatives significantly. For example, the inability of one person to attend the first meeting may be good enough reason to reschedule the meeting. That person's presence may turn the tide in one direction or another at the very beginning.

Principle 3: Identity is referenced in meaning-making and decisions

A living system reproduces and regulates itself from its existing parts and with reference to its identity. Within a human, that identity is physically DNA, and psychologically the sense of self – our stories.

Within an organisational context, Margaret Wheatley (1999) first introduced us to the idea that the organisation's identity is its **purpose, vision and values**. There exists a strong leverage in connecting each employee to these elements so that they may make appropriate, cohesive decisions in their daily work that serve the organisation well. The cohesion is also a source of emergent self-organisation, which we will discuss in Principle 4. In my experience, as you do so, you will also reap the benefits of a better engaged workforce. This connection to purpose and values can be transformational for people and organisation together. I will identify how to do this in Chapter 7.

Employees watch those people in positions of authority carefully. They are looking for consistency between spoken messages and behavioural messages. Any inconsistency fuels scepticism about the spoken message. Although walking the talk is difficult at times (we are all only human), authority figures really need to try. The higher profile that they possess means that the position is a reference point that can be **leveraged**, within the system. It can work for you or against you.

Principle 4: Self-organisation emerges with broad participation

Self-organisation that exists within living systems is a wonder to behold in nature. A common example used to illustrate this quality is the starling murmuration – the name for a flock of starlings. It's called a murmuration because of the sound it makes – a continuous murmur, as the birds flock together and make the most incredible, free-flowing patterns in the sky and even on the ground as they feed.

For a long time, scientists could not work out who was leading the beautiful and very complex pattern formation. (It's interesting that we assume that a bird or a few birds would be leading the way – a mental model.) Eventually, through modelling the behaviour in computer simulations, scientists discovered something incredible. The patterns are formed emergently as each starling follows a simple rule. Each starling seeks to match the direction and speed of its nearest seven or so neighbours (Wood & Beale 2019). It's as simple as that!

No one starling predesigns or has an intention for a specific pattern to emerge. This is an example of **self-organisation where simple rules generate complex emergent behaviour**.

Dee Hock employed the principles of self-organisation when he founded Visa. Hock's ideas were perhaps well before his time, and he was described as a maverick by others. He was in a position to be so influential because of the success of his management style in smaller banks. His basic management principle was to do things *"as conditions, common sense, and ingenuity combined to suggest"* (Hock 1995, p. 2). This principle may seem endearingly simple; however, this simplicity went on to deliver outstanding results because of what he perceived as being common sense. Visa has become an international giant in financial circles that has transformed the way we exchange money.

Hock drew upon the capacity of self-organisation often. For example, on one occasion his company was faced with the enormous task of getting 100,000 card mailers printed within the 12 hours that the mainframe computer was available. Brand new computing and printing technology arrived – and failed. The suppliers of the technology left in embarrassment. Hock relates the story where he and his colleagues inspired each other to develop make-shift innovations that got the job done.

> *We call everyone in the area together, printing company executives, bank officers, programmers, operators, janitors – everyone. There is no need for blame. Will they work the night – no bosses – no procedures – just grab a piece of the problem and get it done? Need help, ask – want to help, offer. Yes? Good! Two people lift a roll of mailers and the printer begins to chatter. Two others grab a second broom handle and begin to roll up mailers as they emerge. Ideas pour out from everyone and someone is instantly on the way to attend to each. "Search the building and steal broom handles." "Get food and drinks sent in." "We'll need gloves." "Round up relief crews." "Rig a backup printer." No one knows all that is happening and no one has time to care. We must trust.*

> *The last roll comes off the printer at six in the morning. An exhausted, happy band of brothers and sisters head home to catch a few hours of sleep before the next ordeal begins.*

As we labored through the night, someone had not only claimed ownership of every aspect of the night's work, but future work separating and folding mailers to get the project back on track. Is that how the future happens? Ingenuity? Passion? Spontaneous order out of chaos? It seems so, as long as control is kept on a leash.

(Hock 2005, pp. 910–917)

This is a small example, but if you look carefully, it demonstrates a process that embraced a shared purpose, people's intrinsic motivations, and experiments to learn what works.

Your organisation is already experiencing self-organisation. The organisational culture with its embedded, usually unspoken values, which have stood the test of time, teaches people what is expected, and they act according to those rules (Schein 1990, p. 111). It is important to be aware that self-organisation already exists within your organisation, and it is beyond control.

Does broad participation mean involving everyone?

The other point that needs to be made clearly here is the importance of broad participation. Self-organisation as described above involved everyone in the situation in different roles. But it doesn't require involving or consulting everyone about every single thing. Each issue requires being thoughtful and deliberate about engaging as broadly as appropriate for each particular issue.

Broad participation is about more than consultation. It's about engaging at a level that draws out the perspectives required to enable the emergence of new solutions or experiments, to make progress on the issue at hand. Identifying whom to involve and how broadly is a matter of judgement and experience, and the tools in Chapter 7 will guide you. But if in doubt, as a general principle, go more broadly rather than less. You can always draw back in more narrowly if required, but once you have set a process in motion with a small and exclusive group, the initial starting conditions have been affected. Other peoples' perceptions have been impacted. Your trust may even be eroded by different views about your motivation.

Think of the flow of information like the flow of blood in your body

Finally, this brings us to the last point about information. We are used to organisations where information is available on a need-to-know basis and is sometimes hoarded as a way of protecting power. If you are seeking to enable adaptation that is appropriate and free flowing, then allow information to flow like blood around a body. Restricted blood flow causes problems!

To take the metaphor further, information is like the nutrients and oxygen that is distributed to our bodies by our blood. Without this nutrition, our body ceases to function. It stands to reason that within an organisation, the more you can share, the better. Enable people to have the data and knowledge they need to make sound and fruitful decisions.

One of my client organisations has gone to the extent of educating their team leaders in basic financial literacy so that they can read and understand the business profit and loss and balance sheets. The intention is to make this information freely available so that better decisions can be made.

Sharing information can be deeply confronting because it challenges so many of our mental models and cultural norms around power. **Transparency** raises issues of who is paid what and invites conversations about fairness. It calls upon the highest integrity of those in authority.

In ethics classes we sometimes talk about the sunlight test. We ask: 'Would this decision survive if we subjected it to the light of day for all to observe it and pass judgement on it?' Organisationally, transparency – sharing information – is a deeply adaptive issue as we move from control to liberation.

Principle 5: Novelty within the system

A living system may adapt in response to novel ideas from within the system – not just information from outside the system.

Just as you read this book and make sense of some new ideas by connecting with what you already know, your brain is making new neural pathways. Novelty, or a new idea, may be emerging within you.

You may then share your new ideas with others. If your new ideas are as different as say, Dee Hock's, you may find yourself ridiculed or ostracised within the organisation. That does not mean retreat; that means you need to find a way to protect yourself as you engage with adaptive work within the system. Attack from others may mean that you are on track!

Now consider those people who are labelled troublemakers or difficult – every organisation has them. They could be expressing the views of the next Dee Hock. How do you know? If you hold the interests of the wellbeing of the whole organisation in mind, what is the value that these sometimes dissenting and sometimes outlandish views bring? What possibilities do they hold?

It may be easy to shut down dissenting views, but is it wise? A guiding principle for your leadership as a change agent might be to hold your own mind open and to **protect the voices of dissidents**. You do not know what or when they may bear fruit. Emergence takes its own path in its own time.

Appreciating divergent voices has implications for nurturing an environment where different views abound and also recruiting a **diversity** of people to offer those different perspectives. And in doing so, you will also nurture the **resilience** of your team – another emergent quality of a living system. The greater the diversity and interconnectivity of your people, the more resilient your organisation will be.

Summing up

In this chapter we have identified the principles, derived from an understanding of living systems, that you can use to underpin the way in which you nurture people and cultivate the conditions for adaptation. They are not a step-by-step recipe of what to do, but rather a range of principles to weigh up within the context of your challenge and organisation.

The Newtonian paradigm is very seductive. It may lure you into believing you have the answers and that your knowledge is common sense.

The relationships between different parts of the system are not static or inanimate. Think of them as **moving energy**. The relationships are either dampening or reinforcing patterns that exist in the system, and the patterns are constantly changing over time because the system has the capacity to adapt. Adaptive or living systems are in constant flux. Take time to seek to understand these dynamics.

Finally, before you begin, become clearer about what you are trying to achieve. Is it a simple goal like killing mosquitoes? This is a reductionist approach and will doom you before you start. Focus on an **intention to bring greater health and wholeness** to the living system.

In the next chapter, we examine some of the mental models we hold around hero leaders. We explore control as a central issue in shifting to a more facilitative type of leadership of change – one that knows that it doesn't know the answers and can't control the outcomes.

Reflection questions

1. Applying the principles in this chapter, what would your team, or organisation, look like, sound like, feel like, if it were as healthy as possible?

    _____

    _____

    _____

    _____

    _____

    _____

2. What may be holding you back from enabling this full expression of a healthy system?

    _____

    _____

    _____

    _____

    _____

    _____

CHAPTER 5

Letting go of the hero leader

To usefully employ the principles of leadership that I described in Chapter 4, you will find that you need to let go of some existing ideas and expectations that you may have about:

- who is a leader

- what is expected of them

- the need to control people to deliver predetermined outcomes.

This letting go is a part of your own adaptation. This chapter is devoted to helping you become more aware of and make that shift within yourself.

A brief history of the hero leader, power and control

A quick historical review of the development of leadership from an Anglo-Saxon perspective reveals a close association between the concepts of power, authority and leadership. The first leaders were kings with God-given authority, and that authority to rule was typically enforced with brute force. Some kings assumed their rule through the use of their armies; however, this was also seen as the will of God. Leadership meant giving orders, being obeyed, being privileged, and ruling by fear of retribution if people didn't obey – either now or in the next lifetime. Were followers taken in consideration? Not really, they didn't matter very much and were seen as a largely expendable resource. Leaders were directive, demanding and controlling – and they were rare and rarefied. There were mystical qualities surrounding these people who were born to rule and favoured by God.

In the middle ages, the power of kings (and some queens) began to diminish as some of their power was distributed to a parliament of the people. The people with power in parliament did not come from a divine line of kings, and the question arose at that time: Who gives authority to the parliament? In 1762 Jean-Jacques Rousseau, a Genevan philosopher, writer and composer who also influenced the Enlightenment, answered this question. In his book *The Social Contract*, he identified that authority came from the people, who agreed to give up some personal freedom in exchange for security and safety. In Heifetz, Groashow and Linsky's adaptive leadership framework, which distinguishes between authority and the exercise of leadership, this unwritten social contract is said to exist for the services of authority. These services are identified as **direction, order and protection** (Heifetz, Grashow & Linsky 2009). In return for these services, people authorise their leaders and allow them to control or strongly influence their futures.

Interest in leadership exploded after the Second World War, as businesses expanded globally. The experiences of the military were a major source of inspiration, and particularly in the area of strategy, the language of a military campaign was adopted. The role of a leader in this context was clearly aligned with the services of authority – telling people what needed to be done and ensuring that it was done. Our current hierarchies still function with command and control at their core.

It wasn't long before research was undertaken into **great men** (and they were men), to identify the traits and the behaviours that brought them such success. This research revered the great men, who also became known as **hero leaders**, in ways that are similar to the mystery that surrounded earlier kings. The notion of a key man who was the source of the inspiring vision and courageous action that won the day was an underlying assumption. Not much time was spent researching the conditions or people surrounding this key person. The assumption of the hero leader continues, and it fits very neatly into the Newtonian paradigm of direct cause and effect.

Sharon Daloz Parks explored the question of what constitutes leadership and whether it can be taught. She identified how our film culture feeds the notion of the hero leader with characters such as Indiana Jones and, more recently, Marvel comic movies. She also argues that the hero leader may have served us well in less complex times when it was possible for one person to know the answers. However, like many other authors today, she argues that as we are confronted with more complex challenges on a greater geographical scale, a new way of understanding the idea of leadership is required and she explores a more distributed and participative leadership such as we explored in Chapter 4 (Parks 2005).

Where does the need for control come from?

There are two sources of control: individual and organisational.

I am very much aware of my struggle with my need for control. It seems that humans all grapple with different degrees of needing control. Being aware of our desire for control is, however, a crucial step towards being liberated from its impact.

What do I mean by **control**? We are all complex beings, and many different needs and values motivate us. Amongst these needs is a spectrum of control varying from weak to strong. The reasons for this desire for power often stem back into childhood or other experiences that may have produced strongly negative emotions. No one wants unpleasant experiences – well, not many of us – and so to protect ourselves, it's natural to seek to control what happens around us.

However, there is also an organisational source of control that layers on top of our individual need for control. As we have just explored how most traditional organisations have evolved from the Newtonian assumption that we can control what occurs, it comes as no surprise that most organisations are designed to control outcomes and people as a way of achieving results. Most people assume that there is no other way.

Managers in their supervisory role over employees have positional or authoritarian power. The employment contract is legally known as a servant–master contract. The impact of this term may only be unconscious. Still, it is powerful, as it often influences employees to consider what they say carefully – lest speaking up be a career-limiting move! Fear can exist as an unintended consequence of these arrangements.

Shifting from production line businesses to knowledge-based activities has been a catalyst for learning how to improve performance through engaging each worker's capability to think for themselves rather than following instructions in minute detail. As a part of this development, managers have been learning how to get things done without using their authority and controlling outcomes. They are beginning to learn that control does not enable creativity, learning or adaptation very well at a time when competitive advantage is seen to exist within these capacities.

Letting go of control is crucial

My intention is to raise your awareness around how deeply and unconsciously we have absorbed the Newtonian paradigm's assumption of a linear, predictable and therefore controllable world into the everyday operation of our businesses. It pervades recruitment, performance review, strategic planning, management by objectives, and change management processes. But it doesn't need to.

If you stop and reflect for a moment, it is likely that you are also observing the new paradigm emerging within your organisation too. Indicators of this include the use of external coaches, the emergence of managers learning to coach their staff, a growing concern with employee satisfaction and engagement, and greater consultation around changes.

The Newtonian and living systems paradigms are co-existing in organisations today; however, the Newtonian paradigm is more dominant and will remain so until senior management and boards let go of the need to control and instead focus on trusting and liberating their people.

New structures that decentralise decision making, such as Frederic Laloux's teal organisations (Laloux 2014) and holocracy practices, are emerging to enable liberation in a responsible fashion. I am not, however, advocating for a change in your organisational structure at present. That is a discussion for another time and place. I am advocating that you be aware of the power and control dynamic and your own need for it. It is the power and control dynamic that accompanies authority that often dampens the possibility of emergent change. This occurs either because of your own need to cling to your answer or other people's response to authority by not speaking up.

Importantly, you can shape an island of trust within your own team with an awareness of the dynamic of underlying control within the organisation. You can manage around it. I have witnessed hierarchical organisations become more aware of the need to liberate rather than control.

Change will flow naturally when managers let go of control and enable the natural human forces of growth and development to be liberated.

The unrecognised price of control

There is a price associated with control that is rarely recognised.

My observation is that it is possible to obtain a sense of control over short time frames and within close geographical distances. For example, my to-do list for today may start with a sense of control in the morning, but often by the end of the day it has spiralled out of control as the day has presented interruptions that I didn't predict or expect. If I control my day rigidly, I may not respond appropriately to those interruptions that are actually different forms of opportunities. And there is a price to be paid for this control – the loss of possibilities.

On a scale broader than the to-do list, the price of control is self-limitation because of sole reliance on our own perspective, and not engaging other people's creativity and initiative to respond to opportunities as plans unfold. Other people's energy is not fully liberated when we control. Just recall how you feel when you have to do something, but you don't agree with it or own it. Moreover, under the strong influence of control, the plan restricts those implementing it to what is within the plan. And the plan can in no way anticipate every nuance of the future. Opportunities that arise outside the plan are often not spotted and not capitalised upon.

We desire control personally and organisationally – to achieve specific outcomes. The two paradigms we have explored to date suggest that control may be possible if our organisations truly are machines – but they are not. The science of living systems suggests that people, organisations and society may be better understood to function according to the behaviours of living systems. If this is the case, then control without cost within organisations was and is an illusion.

The alternative is not an organisation in which people are irresponsible or unaccountable. In fact, my experience has been quite the opposite – I have seen people become more engaged and accountable. These outcomes flow from leadership that is exercised differently than in the hero leader model. It begins with a different way of perceiving and is mirrored by different personal qualities that the person exercising leadership chooses to exhibit. That is what we will look at next – the second layer in the Big Little Shift framework (Figure 2).

Reflection questions

1. How aware are you personally of your desire for control?

_____

_____

_____

_____

2. How strong is the need for control organisationally?

_____

_____

_____

_____

3. How much do your people trust you? How do you know?

_____

_____

_____

_____

4. What might you do to reduce the control over people and increase the sense of trust they have in you and their organisation?

_____

_____

_____

_____

CHAPTER 6

Introducing the leader as gardener

For those who study how to lead change, it has become crystal clear that **who the change agent is being** matters. I am referring to your being; how people perceive you, how you engage with people, how you make them feel. It matters more than what the change agent knows – because the change agent can't know the answer. This insight is summed up by Dunphy, Griffiths & Benn (2007) as:

> *What do we need to be effective change leaders? We need clarity of vision, knowledge of what we wish to change and the skills to implement the changes. But none of these can be fully effective without maturity and wisdom. In the end it is who we are, not what we know or can do, that makes the crucial difference in effecting organizational change.* (p.293).

When it comes to leading adaptive or transformational change, your personal qualities are a crucial success factor. The question of your personal development is worth your attention, and this small chapter does not do it justice. In a sense, it can't do it justice because your personal development is something you need to attend to constantly, and it is largely experiential. I strongly encourage you to spend as much of your resources as you can forever pushing your own boundaries of self-awareness as you interact with others and extend your capacity for understanding how you are seen by others. As you do so, you will also experience increased self-satisfaction as you gain improved outcomes through your interactions with others.

In the preceding chapter, we explored the notion of control, and the most powerful alternative for this is being a person who intends to **liberate possibilities** within the system. Liberating possibilities is the dynamic of adaptive change and the initial focus of this chapter before I introduce a new metaphor for a leader – the leader as gardener – and five qualities that you could nurture within yourself.

An energetic transformation from within you

In 2000, Ben Zander, the musical director of the Boston Philharmonic Orchestra, co-authored a book with Rosamund Stone Zander, a professional coach (Zander & Zander 2000). It contains simple principles to guide a professional and personal transformational journey. These principles support your ability to generate an internal energetic shift in yourself – a shift to being someone who has let go of control and who liberates possibilities.

I have summarised the lessons from the Zanders' book in Table 4. I am not going to go through each principle – that would be a book in itself – as indeed it is! I do recommend that you read this book or watch a video clip of Ben Zander. The energetic shift is a result of living these principles, and they are entirely compatible with the principles of living systems that were identified in Chapter 4.

Table 4: Zanders' leadership principles for liberating possibility (adapted from Zander & Zander 2000)

Principle	Explanation
Speak possibility	Recognise when conversations head into a downward spiral of negativity, and turn those conversations around to discuss possibilities.
Look for and generate shining eyes	An indicator of people being excited about the possibilities is that their eyes are shining.
Enrol every voice into the vision	Be inclusive and discover the visions that other people hold too.
Lead by making others powerful	Illustrated by the observation that the conductor of an orchestra does not make a sound.
Quiet the voice in the head that says 'I can't do it...'	That's the voice in your head and the voice in everyone else's head too.
Everyone gets an A	Rather than judging people, let everyone be an A – a possibility for them to live into rather than a standard to live up to.
Remember rule #6	Rule #6 is not to take yourself too seriously. Life is for living and enjoying.

The fundamental question for you to consider as a change agent is this: How alive are you and others to the possibilities of life? As many climate scientists, for example, have learned the hard way, being a leader who is highly analytical and with rational reasons for change is not sufficient. It can be necessary, but it is never enough.

How can you be a person who breathes life into new possibilities? That means that you need to be someone who holds your own answers and solutions lightly. Your own sense of joy at the heart of the prospect of the change journey needs to shine through for people. You are inviting them into the experience of life itself. Adaptation is a possibility because we are alive!

Adaptation is a possibility to change something (even an accounts payment system, for example) that leaves a legacy for others. This adaptation to new technology or a greater insight into the needs of customers is a possibility to serve others. These possibilities enable us all the opportunity to employ our personal strengths in ways that we will learn and grow from. It will enable us to connect to a sense of purpose. It's an opportunity to rewrite our own life stories and recreate each of us too. And when we are successful, we might notice 'people with shining eyes'. A brilliant indicator of being engaged and alive.

I would love to be in the room with you now, because I want you to feel the energetic shift that this idea of radiating possibilities brings with it. The difference in the energy that you bring to people will have a strong impact on them. Research from the Institute of HeartMath shows that as we are in close proximity to others, our hearts share electromagnetic fields (McCraty, Atkinson & Tomasino 2001). We can literally feel or sense each other in this way.

Your energy (or being) will influence others. Your energy has the potential to transform others. Be mindful of the energy that you are projecting. As we progress through this book, we are going to become quite intellectual or heady – so, write down somewhere in big letters...

Radiate possibility with my energy!

Find ways of turning on your possibility-radiating energy when you need it most. It might be by listening to particular music, rubbing your feet in the grass, or meditation. Identify and use your ways.

Five qualities to nurture within yourself to cultivate change

With that sense of radiating possibility as an energic foundation, I wish to share with you a summary that my colleague Sam Wells and I recently developed. Firstly, we identified a new metaphor, the **leader as gardener**, to replace the hero leader. We then identified five qualities that change agents – those who wish to cultivate (garden) adaptation – might nurture within themselves to cultivate the conditions for emergent change (Wells & McLean 2020, in press).

The leader as gardener emerged as a new alternative way of thinking about the role of a change agent in a complex environment.

The leader as gardener does not lead from the front, knowing answers and providing the services of authority. Consistent with the principles identified in Chapter 4, the leader as gardener is a facilitative leader from anywhere within the organisation who:

- identifies an adaptive challenge

- brings people together to understand the challenge

- experiments in ways that make progress on the challenge.

The gardener nurtures or cultivates the conditions for learning and adaptation rather than leading or driving change. These expressions – leading or driving change – are a result of the Newtonian way of understanding the way the world works. They assume direct and linear cause and effect.

Humility

In stark contrast to the hero leader, the gardener is vulnerable and says, 'I don't know the answer to this complex challenge' (see Principle 2 in Chapter 4). The gardener also encourages others to recognise that they too don't know, and that the way forward involves everyone learning together. There is vulnerability and wisdom in recognising and admitting that we don't know, and that we can learn more.

Trust

Placing the challenge at the feet of the system, so to speak, requires trust in the capacity of the people involved to find a way forward together – a trust in their individual capacities and their capacity to work together. As detailed in Chapter 5, the gardener lets go of the need for control and trusts the system to resolve the challenge over time. The gardener is still a part of that system and has influence within it, but the gardener is very careful not to diminish the opportunities for co-creation and emergence within the system. The system as a whole will learn its way towards solutions, or at least make progress on the issue.

Patience

Very often in our current organisational climates we value immediate action over anything else. We tend to ask 'How long do we have to undertake a task?' and squeeze it into the time available. Research shows people are feeling increasingly stressed and overwhelmed (Symes 2014), and while people are so overwhelmed, there is no time for undertaking anything more than single-loop learning.

Patience is required for the process of listening to perspectives, understanding the issues in all their complexity, and learning the way forward together. Adaptation happens in its own good time. It will not be rushed – much. As a manager, it is possible to pace the work a little, but all in all, patience is required.

Adaptation will be messier and take longer than most people desire. Patience is required as an aggressive virtue, as my colleague often says. If you surrender to the temptation to push things along and take control, you will not obtain the gains you desire.

Being patient is **not doing nothing**. Being patient is providing time and space for the necessary learning and change to work its way through people. Patience reflects your trust in the system.

Vision

Leadership is inseparable from the idea of a picture of a better future in some way. But the question for the leader as gardener is 'Whose vision?' Given our preceding exploration of living systems and the need for humility and trust, the vision cannot be the gardener's vision imposed on others.

The gardener nurtures the conditions in which people can co-create a shared vision. This shared vision enables an inclusive view of possibilities from different perspectives and enlivens each person's ownership of the issue and its resolution. The co-created vision generates a sense of a joint quest. We will return to this idea in Chapter 7 when I will describe how to generate such a shared vision, even with large groups of people.

Awareness of the broader system

This particular quality or awareness is very difficult to describe in writing, and it is what I am seeking to help you develop. It is described by some as an intuition and by others as a broader or deeper level of awareness of the condition of the system. Sometimes it is described as a feeling. Donella Meadows (2008) describes it as both quantitative data and a sense of how the system is feeling that provides a sense of the beat of the system.

By 'system' I mean those elements that exist within the system of interest – that sphere of concern and influence that is required to make a difference to the particular adaptive issue that has been identified. In Chapter 7 I will identify some tools that will help you observe and interpret what is happening within the system of interest.

Chapter 10 will identify some practices to help hone your 'gardening' skills, but at this time I want to emphasise the helpfulness of the simple practice of being reflective.

Reflection questions

Cultivate your own self-awareness with questions such as:

1. What happened in that interaction? What were the outcomes?

    _____

    _____

    _____

2. What did I expect the outcomes to be?

    _____

    _____

    _____

3. How did I contribute to the outcomes? How did my personal strengths and limitations play out in this context?

    _____

    _____

    _____

4. What have I learned about me and others?

    _____

    _____

    _____

5. How is my sense of identity evolving?

    _____

    _____

    _____

CHAPTER 7

How to prepare yourself for action

Having explored the first two layers of Figure 2, we now enter the more pragmatic section of the book. Chapters 7–10 offer guiding frameworks, tools, skills and practices. It is possible that once you have embodied the worldview offered by the very first two layers – perceiving the world through the lens of the paradigm of complexity – you can operate without consciously employing the guiding tools provided in the remaining chapters. As you are developing the embodiment, however, the tools and frameworks can be very helpful in guiding your own adaptive transformation.

Exercising your leadership for adaptation

The structure of this section could be construed as paradoxical, because I am about to offer you a linear looking process for a non-linear activity. Figure 6 identifies this process, and this chapter discusses Elements 1–4, while Chapter 8 discusses Elements 5–6 and Chapter 9 enables us to reflect on Element 7. These are categorised by the intention behind each element. Elements 1–4 are focused on understanding what your adaptive issue is, while Elements 5–7 focus on getting into action. I have deliberately chosen to call parts of the process elements rather than stages, to avoid reinforcing the linear appearance of the process.

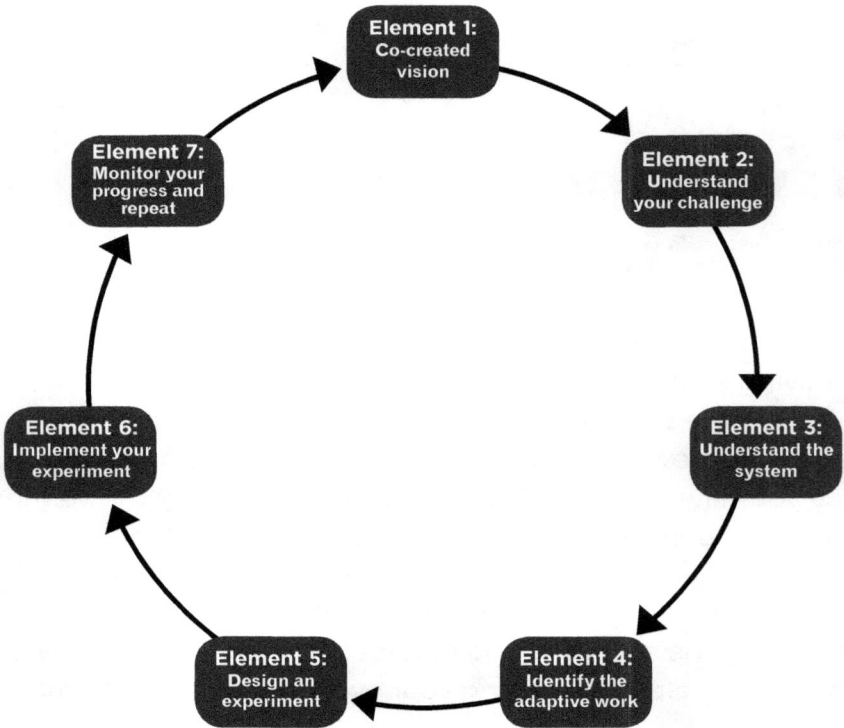

Figure 6: Seven elements of cultivating adaptive and transformational change

From a pragmatic perspective, you could start anywhere in the process in Figure 6. It could be that you are already intervening in a system as you read this book. For example, you might recognise that you are currently at Element 3 and that your natural next step is to think about what you want to achieve (Element 1) as you begin to move into Element 4. That simple example also illustrates how you might jump about within the process too, and that is natural.

Adaptive work is always messy, so don't be surprised if that is the way you experience the process of working with it. Figure 6 is only a guide, and as you proceed you may find that you want to backtrack to earlier elements to redo portions of the process. There are never right answers that emerge from each element; think of your analysis producing ideas to test.

As I am writing about this process in a linear fashion, however, it seems that the best place to start is to follow one of Steven Covey's enduring principles (from his best seeling book *The 7 habits of highly effective people*) and **begin with the end in mind**.

And although Covey's advice is sound, it is important to remember that in a living system, there is no end. There is no destination. This is because a living system is in a state of continuous evolution. So, starting with the end in mind might better be expressed as considering what your issue will be like when your work is done well enough for another challenge to become a higher priority.

Element 1: Identify your co-created vision and purpose

How often do you notice people debating what should be done and how? Or leaping into action without much thought about why they are taking action? It seems to be a very human trait to leap into action. This trait is not aided by our increasingly busy organisational lives, where we have honed the efficiency of the business to such an extent that many workers report that they are close to burnout and constantly rushing.

If we want different outcomes, we need to do things differently – and envisioning is the first thing to do. It's actually not such a different thing to do; we just seem to have forgotten its power and relevance to leadership for some reason. Within hectic workplaces, a call to stop and begin an important change process with an envisioning session can be met with some resistance. Even asking people to stop and clarify what they want from a particular conversation appears difficult at times.

What makes envisioning uncomfortable?

I first became conscious of the tendency to shy away from visions when I read the work of Donella Meadows, a former Massachusetts Institute of Technology (MIT) systems dynamics modeller. Meadows was an analytical woman by training who, as she worked with people around complex problems, learned the power of vision. As she worked with people on complex problems, she learned why we often tend to shy away from it. Her list includes beliefs that we within our Western culture tend to hold that visions are:

- fantasies and unrealistic

- dangerous (e.g. Hitler had a vision)

- childish or naïve in nature.

Meadows also observed that strangers are often willing to complain bitterly to each other about what is wrong, but when it comes to sharing what they really want the future to be like, they are quieter. It seems that it can be embarrassing for people to reveal what they want in an ideal world. They can feel quite intimidated to reveal their idealism after years of being taught to be realistic and practical.

Warming people to the task of envisioning

My experience is that there is benefit in warming people to the task of envisioning. I do this in several ways that you might like to consider trying too.

1. Remind people that they typically use visions all the time. Ask them to reflect on times when they commonly employ a vision even if they don't call it that. For example, planning a new house or holiday with the family.

2. Try altering the language with the term **imagining**.

3. Normalise the sense of vulnerability people might experience as you engage them in this process too.

Typically, after accustoming people to envisioning, participants become very engaged. Together, you will experience the unifying and integrating effect of the emergent shared vision.

Conceptually, envisioning is not about aligning people in one direction

It has long been recognised that a sense of heading in the same direction is desirable. If we are not headed in the same direction, then arguments eventually arise because of hidden assumptions about where each person thinks we are headed. People often think they are going in the same direction, but in fact, each person holds a different view of where that is. The common Newtonian idea of alignment is everyone on the one pathway to the vision. The assumption is that the path to the vision is known and direct. This idea is illustrated in the left-hand side in Figure 7.

Newtonian alignment with assumption of a direct path

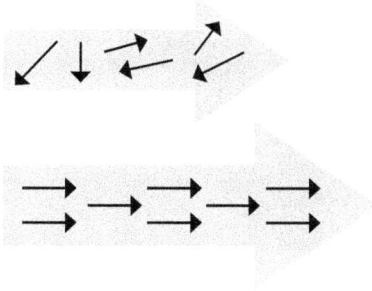

Living Systems connection and learning

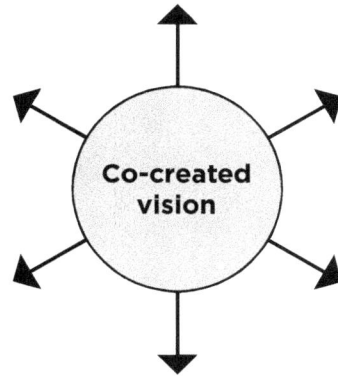

Co-created vision

Figure 7: Contrast between the Newtonian and the living systems notions of cohesive vision

In the paradigm of living systems, the vision is itself acknowledged to be evolving as we learn, and we acknowledge that we don't know the pathway to bring that vision into being. When everyone is engaged with the same shared vision, there may still be different views about how to bring the vision into reality, and these represent valuable different possibilities. The possibilities and resultant experiments are still cohesive by virtue of the shared vision that seeds them. This different way of perceiving the vision in the living systems paradigm is illustrated on the right-hand side of Figure 7.

The co-created vision nurtures a cradle for learning together

The model in Figure 8 introduces another way of viewing this dynamic of learning how to bring the vision into reality. The vision provides a unifying cradle from which we may experiment to learn the way forward.

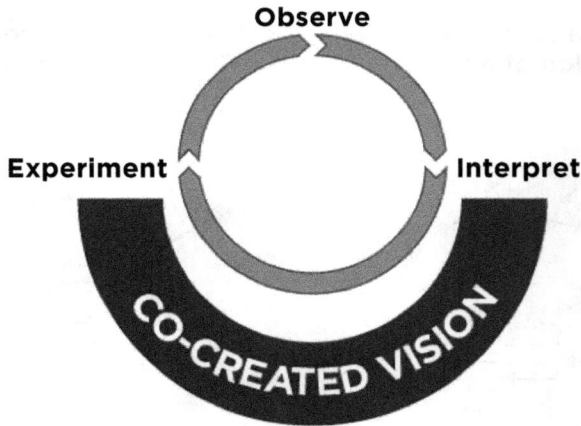

Figure 8: Co-created vision as a cradle for experiments

Heifetz's iterative cycle of Obverse, Interpret and Intervene (Heifetz, Grashow & Linsky 2009) is acknowledged and relabelled in Figure 8. I prefer the term 'Experiment' to 'Intervene', just to remind us that we don't know the answer. We are always running experiments to see what may be learned.

Further, Heifetz's cycle does not mention the cradling influence of a co-created shared vision. Rather, Heifetz's work is developed from the perspective and purpose of one person seeking to influence the system. Although it may still be employed in this manner, the changes that I've included here make progress in teams within organisational and community contexts more obvious.

The process of envisioning together generates cohesion because the process:

- enables people to do their adaptive work as they seek to understand each other's perspectives to generate the shared vision

- nurtures interpersonal relationships and social capital as a result of being vulnerable enough to share their vision and listen to each other

- includes everyone and all views – it does not close options or people down

- reveals values within the shared vision that can be used in decision making

- provides a story that holds the complexity and can be revisited for orientation when ambiguity is high, and motivation when energy inevitably wanes.

The process of envisioning

Envisioning, as a process, is what facilitators call an easy win-win process because it is an **inclusive process** – you will recognise the application of Principles 2 and 3, in particular, from Chapter 4. No one has to justify why they believe a certain element should be included. If it is genuinely important to them – it's in! The rest of the group includes it because one person believes it is important. 'If it's important to you, then it's important to us' is the message.

Identifying what is a viable solution in the longer term occurs as experiments take place after the vision is generated. In this way the voices of the outliers are not lost; they are valued, included and integrated into the vision. **Diversity really is respected and valued.** The diversity within the vision is also important because its inclusion and connection in the integrated vision is a source of resilience within the complex system too.

Another important feature of the co-creation process is that no one needs to say how the vision will be achieved. The envisioning process comprises only the formation of the cradle – not the experiments themselves.

The envisioning process and the question that sits at the centre of it may be tailored for all sorts of situations. My colleague and I have used the process in National Climate Change Adaptation Research Facility (NCCARF) research designed to help Natural Resource Management Boards develop strategies to obtain action on climate change in rural communities (Meyer et al. 2013). The communities envisioned how people really want to experience the landscape (including human communities). I have also used envisioning with a community group seeking to mobilise people in Gumeracha, South Australia, to improve their town's main street. Gumeracha's Main Street Project has become an award-winning inspiration for community action. I have employed envisioning with employees throughout organisations to articulate a shared vision of the organisational culture that they really want. I have employed it with teams to determine the influence they really want to create together. All that is required is a little tweak of the central question. The important elements of the question are as follows.

- Focus the question on what people **really want** rather than what they realistically believe they can achieve. Idealism is pragmatic in a vision! This approach is sometimes called a solution-focused approach.

- Keep attention on **how the situation will be experienced when it is resolved**, rather than the tangible form of the vision. For example, if we were to envision a house, the vision we would generate is about how people will experience that house. The participants may identify qualities such as the house being secure, warm, spacious, energy efficient, comfortable and welcoming, rather than a house with so many square metres of space, a red roof and nine windows. The tangible description is one solution – which in the world of complexity will emerge. You do not yet know the solution, although because we are human, we might think that we do.

At the end of the process you will have a shared story of how you as a group want to experience the challenge when it is resolved. We often divide this story up into paragraphs that represent each of the five to seven core messages also identified in the process. The aim is to have the story fit on one page if possible and accompanied by pictures.

As an illustration, the Gumeracha Main Street Vision is shown in Figure 9 (Gumeracha Main Street, 2017).

You can read more about the envisioning process in the original article (Wells & McLean 2013).

GUMERACHA MAIN STREET VISION

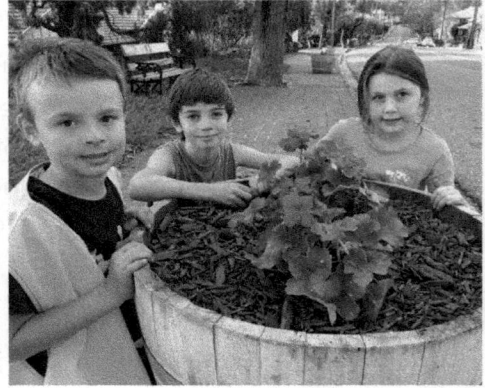

PERAMANGK CULTURE & HARMONY

We are committed to recognising the complete history of our township, knowing and celebrating local Aboriginal culture and developing a two way partnership with Peramangk Peoples for a harmonious future.

FRIENDLY

Gumeracha Main Street is a community space where locals and visitors feel comfortable to enjoy. In businesses and outside it is a space for people of all ages, cultures and backgrounds – everyone is welcome.

NATURE

Gumeracha Main Street is connected to the natural environment. It provides access and visual amenity to the natural beauty that surrounds it. Design elements reflect the close relationship between the street and the world beyond.

ABUNDANCE

We celebrate the produces of local artisans. Fresh food, locally made products and artworks are available in businesses on the street and public spaces reflect the community and its abundant offerings.

LINGER

Gumeracha Main Street is a place to spend time for leisure, business and community. It provides places to meet, stop, shop and play.

DISCOVERY

The Main Street has a character of its own. There are elements of surprise and an allure to explore and discover the heart and history of the township.

UNINHIBITED

Gumeracha Main Street is not limited by convention. It respects heritage while embracing new and exciting elements which make it stand out from the crowd. Art is celebrated and shared and good design is considered in all aspects.

SAFE

Gumeracha Main Street is a place where everyone feels safe – whether that's crossing the road, walking at night or splashing in puddles. Spaces are designed with consideration for all users of the street – from the very young to the very old.

Figure 9: Example of a completed shared vision
(reprinted from Gumeracha Main Street Project, 2017)

EXERCISE: Envisioning

Allocate half an hour with 4–6 people involved in resolving your challenge to share your individual stories about how you each want to experience the adaptive challenge when it is resolved. Then develop a shared story that each person believes includes their story. Practise retelling this story to ensure you all have a shared understanding of it. Notice the most important values in your co-created story. The whole exercise will take approximately an hour.

Element 2: Observe and interpret: seek to understand

Although shown as two elements in Figure 8, **observing** and **interpreting** almost always occur simultaneously. To separate them into different elements requires you to recognise your own process of perception in the moment of observation. It also requires you to be like a blank slate with regard to your own personal biases and mental models. Given that every human brain functions by storing information in the form of mental models, it is almost impossible not to interpret as you observe.

My colleague Sam Wells often uses this example in his MBA classes. Imagine walking into a business you have not come into contact with before. You enter the front reception area and notice the work area arranged in an open office style. You let the receptionist know that you are here to meet with the CEO, and you are ushered over to a corner where the CEO's desk is – amongst everyone else. Together you walk to a closed meeting room to talk. There is a background buzz as people go about their work, but it's not noisy, and everyone seems to be engaged.

How do you interpret this office layout? Why is it like it is? What do you think it suggests? Stop and actually think this through before reading on. What do you assume as a result of the observation shared so far?

One interpretation might be that the CEO is a new age woman, appreciating an egalitarian approach where everyone can talk to everyone else. The CEO, although having a greater position of authority, is a worker, the same as everyone else. This layout might also suggest easy and open sharing of information, resulting in quick decision making. Everyone is able to access exactly what they want, and they need to be highly agile!

Here's another possible interpretation.

The CEO and board have experienced fraud in the past and suffered a great deal from it. The business nearly went broke! Now processes and systems are in place to control everything and everyone. No one in this office can even go to the toilet without someone else knowing about it! Everyone is being watched all the time, and an open office layout enables that outcome. Trust no one!

There are numerous interpretations, and I wonder what interpretation you made. The point is to notice that there are in fact numerous possibilities – and that we are drawn to our own conclusions, often unconsciously, and very quickly. We usually don't even notice that we are applying our own mental models. Research studying just how quickly people make snap judgements of other people, founded on mental models, suggests it could be as quick as 50 milliseconds (Rule 2014).

The world of systems thinking provides a great tool to help us understand ourselves and attempt to separate our observations from our snap interpretation. This is called the **ladder of inference** (Figure 10) (Argyris 1990, p 88-89). It shows how we move from data to a selection that reinforces our existing view of the challenge, to which we add our own meaning, make assumptions and draw conclusions before we decide what action to take. The ladder of inference can be thought of as a pictorial illustration of how our mental models work to become self-fulfilling prophecies.

Talking through the ladder of inference with colleagues can help us understand the lightning-fast process of meaning-making we all employ. It can help us to question what data we are taking notice of and what data we might not even be noticing, and to examine the unconscious meaning that we are adding.

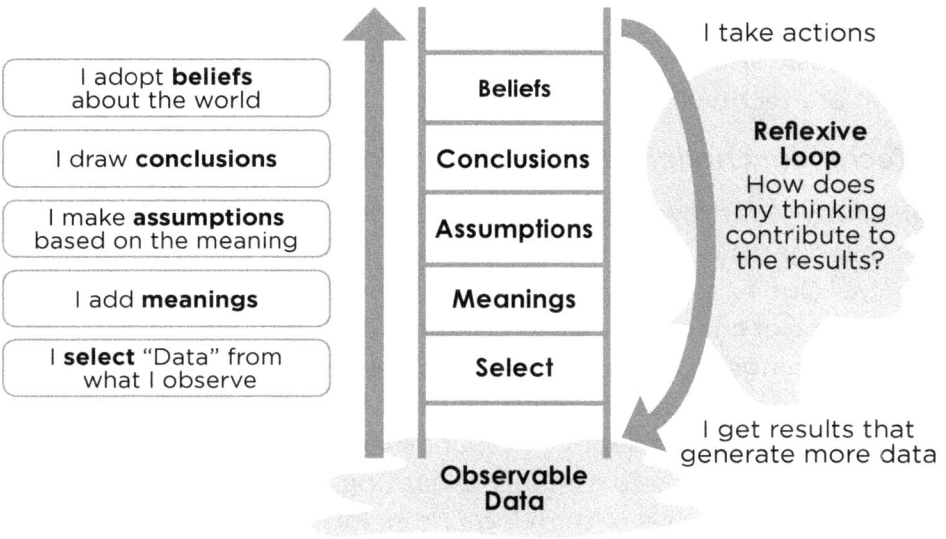

| I adopt **beliefs** about the world |
| I draw **conclusions** |
| I make **assumptions** based on the meaning |
| I add **meanings** |
| I **select** "Data" from what I observe |

Beliefs

Conclusions

Assumptions

Meanings

Select

Observable Data

I take actions

Reflexive Loop
How does my thinking contribute to the results?

I get results that generate more data

Figure 10: The ladder of inference (adapted from Hutchens, 1999, p72)

Understanding the challenge before rushing in

Donella Meadows (2008) advises us to **get the beat of the system**.

> *Before you disturb the system in any way, watch how it behaves. If it's a piece of music or a whitewater rapid or a fluctuation in a commodity price, study its beat. If it's a social system, watch it work. Learn its history.* (p. 170)

Keep good records, Meadows advises, because you can't always rely on memory.

> *Focus on facts, not theories. It keeps you from falling too quickly into your own beliefs or misconceptions, or those of others . . . I have been told with great authority that the milk price was going up when it was going down, that real interest rates were falling when they were rising.*

(pp. 170–171)

Getting the beat is what the next two exercises are all about. It involves gaining an understanding of the system and its interdependencies. You will become aware of plenty of interconnections as you begin with the apparently simple yet not easy task of considering your issue in terms of those elements that are technical in nature and those that are adaptive.

Technical challenges involve single-loop learning

Heifetz, Grashow and Linsky (2009) describes a technical challenge as one that we can clearly identify and know how to solve. Our expectation can be that the solution fixes the issue. This type of challenge doesn't require us to think or feel differently about things in order for the problem to be solved. A technical challenge is a situation where single-loop learning will do the job. In some cases, an adaptive challenge may have become technical over time. It is possible that the learning has already been done, revealing new ways of thinking and doing that have resulted in a solution that will fix the challenge.

Adaptive challenges involve double- or triple-loop learning

An adaptive challenge, on the other hand, is one that requires double-loop learning. It requires us to reveal and challenge our unconscious assumptions or mental models to ourselves and others. As previously mentioned, Heifetz, Grashow and Linsky (2009) also describes this adaptive work as reprioritising values.

Additionally, you will find yourself needing to undertake your own adaptive and emotional work as the system comes together to consider its adaptive challenges too. Adaptive work is uncomfortable and often makes us feel incompetent because we don't know what the answer is yet. We are in the process of unlearning what we thought we knew and learning again.

Contrast between technical and adaptive work

Think about the nature of a single-loop learning technical challenge, and the way we feel when presented with one.

Usually it is a sense of comfort – we feel like we know what the solution is, so there is a sense of confidence and competence that accompanies the technical challenge. It is easy to appreciate how we mere humans are drawn to see nearly every challenge as technical.

Most challenges, however, are only partially technical. Most challenges have adaptive elements. When these adaptive elements are overlooked, it means that we keep coming up with technical solutions that deal with the adaptive facets of the issue. And the issue keeps reappearing over time. It hasn't been addressed at all – it's still there like a 'slippery little sucker' or mouse under a rug!

Table 5 is an example of a chart I often develop in my workshops with clients as we talk through the difference between technical and adaptive challenges. Of course, these two elements are not as neatly separated as the table suggests. In life and work, most challenges we face are a combination of technical and adaptive challenges, and it may be more appropriate to think of technical and adaptive being on a spectrum.

Table 5: Distinction between technical and adaptive challenges (adapted from O'Malley & Cebula 2015)

	Technical Challenge (single loop)	Adaptive Challenge (double loop)
The problem is...	Clear and known	Unclear (it's a 'slippery little sucker')
The solution is...	Known – no new learning	Unknown – requires lots of new learning
The deliverable is usually...	A tangible output	An intangible outcome
You can expect...	To fix the problem	To make progress on the issue
The timeline is...	Now or ASAP	Longer term (usually longer than expected)
The process will feel...	Neat and tidy	Messy and uncomfortable
A useful attitude to hold is...	Confidence in your competence	Curiosity and a desire to learn
Your response is...	Use your authority and TELL people what needs to be done.	Gather the people in the system together and ASK. Enable new experiments to emerge.

EXERCISE: Understand your challenge

This exercise invites you to understand and analyse your challenge – not to solve it. Observe yourself and others with whom you might undertake this exercise. How quickly does the conversation turn to solutions? Listen very carefully, because solutions can insert themselves very subtly.

I suggest a large piece of butcher's paper. Create two columns, one headed Technical and the other Adaptive. In conversation with others, see if you can tease apart the technical from the adaptive elements of the challenge as it is now. If it is a major issue, I would allow at least an hour for this conversation, and it is likely that you will all find it taxing. It will probably feel as though you are getting nowhere. Which is a good sign because it indicates you are dealing with an adaptive issue.

This simple exercise may even make some progress with your adaptive issue, by employing it with other people. That's because the conversation generates a deeper shared understanding of the different elements implicated in the challenge.

Respond differently to the technical and adaptive elements

Once done, this exercise has another benefit. The technical elements are the places in which you will get some easy and quick wins in progressing your challenge. These are the low-hanging fruit if you like. This is because the technical challenges can be easily addressed – people already perceive in ways that mean you can just tell them what needs to be done and they are able to do that. Put another way, you can use your role or authority to instruct people. If you don't have formal authority, you should find that people will be willing to undertake these tasks – they will be relatively easy.

The list of associated elements on the adaptive side of your sheet of paper now more clearly identifies the nature of your adaptive challenge. These are the challenges where simply telling people what to do will not get the job done. You need to engage people in a process of revealing the mental models and values that sit underneath the way you are perceiving the challenge at present. This is helping you to think more deeply and hypothesise about the adaptive work.

Element 3: Obverse and interpret: understand the challenge within the system

So, we are still in observation mode. Still holding back from leaping in. Notice if you find this frustrating. It's probably your sense of knowing the answer already or viewing the challenge in a technical manner. It's OK. We are all drawn in this direction – just notice it.

Defining the system of interest

Now consider the system of interest or the context within which your challenge exists. Within an organisational setting, it is common to consider the whole organisation as the system of interest. If the organisation is too large, try reducing the system of interest to a division – but beware of the functional silos. Limiting the system of interest to a functional division may mean you are ignoring important parts of the whole. Let me try to explain that last statement with an example from a community setting.

Some clients I work with in the sphere of community issues often have trouble deciding on the size of their system of interest. That's because it is an entirely arbitrary choice. Deciding upon a boundary to a system that is interconnected to everything else is very fuzzy.

For example, if your adaptive issue is concerned with healthy food supply chains within the state you live in, how do you define the system of interest? The decision may rest upon other factors such as your level of political influence or privilege that you enjoy. It may also rest upon the time and resources you have available. I encourage you to experiment with taking a big bird's eye view of the entire state-wide system (which is, of course, a part of the national and international food supply chain). After you have done this, you might like to reduce the size of your system to something that is more local – and as you do this, notice the way in which the local system reflects and is truly a nested sub-system within the whole. All the elements of the whole larger system are also at play within the smaller system of interest, but they may be more accessible at the smaller scale – this is an illustration of the fundamental principle of holonic thinking (introduced in Chapter 3).

My advice is to experiment. Try the next exercise at different scales to determine what is the most useful way for you to perceive and work within the system. I think of it as zooming out and in.

Within an organisational setting, zooming in to one division may remove parts of the whole because of the way an organisation is usually structured as a hierarchy and siloed into functional divisions.

EXERCISE: Your challenge within the system – the pizza

Marty Linsky was teaching a class at Harvard University's Kennedy School of Government, where he introduced the class I was participating in to the idea of a social system expressed as different factions. This analysis was something that Marty referred to in an offhand way as a pizza – because when drawn, it looks like a pizza. In Figure 11, I have provided an example of a pizza based on several different clients, which I will use to explain this tool. More formally, it can be thought of as understanding the political landscape.

Figure 11: Example of the pizza, placing the adaptive issue within the context of the system

It helps to make the pizza with other people's input, but you can complete it on your own too.

Begin by drawing a circle on a large piece of paper. This represents your system of interest. From your analysis to date, place a short description of your central adaptive issue in the centre of the circle. In the example in Figure 11, the issue is 'learning to deliver system changes'. Then begin to add a slice of the pizza for each faction in the system.

Factions are not the same as stakeholders. Factions are groups of people who **think and feel similarly** about the adaptive challenge. There may be a number of factions within one stakeholder group. There may be factions that span across stakeholder groups.

There are two factions that you should always add immediately. These two are yourself or the group you are working with on this challenge, and the main authority figure in the system.

Add yourself as a reminder that you are a part of this system – not separate from it. As a part of the system, you will have to adapt too. Ask yourself: 'What is really at stake in this issue for me/us?' This is a time for brutal honesty with yourself. In the example in Figure 11, the group leading the change (labelled as 'Us') identified different values, including:

• minimum disruption

• their people being 'on-board'

• engaged with the why of the change.

At another, perhaps almost unspeakable level, the group of managers I am imagining may really be saying, 'Don't make life any harder for us. Let's only do the changes we really have to. Keep people happy so we can get on with business as usual.' If they expressed their concerns in this way at work, they may be seen as being obstructive in the organisation. They may not even want to admit this to themselves – that they are a part of what others may call resistance to change.

You may not want to share your personal motivations with others, but be as brutally honest with yourself as you can in this process. Think of **yourself as a system within the system** (a holon – right?). Consider your loyalties to other people – maybe those whom you are trying to influence. Your level of self-awareness will help you notice those mental models that are influencing the way in which you perceive and frame the challenge. In turn, your awareness will help you act with integrity and be more effective.

The second automatic inclusion within your pizza is the major authority figure within your system of interest. What this person thinks and says either supports your cause or doesn't. You need to know what this person thinks and feels about your specific issue. If you don't know, then you probably need to discover what this person is thinking. Amongst everything else they think of, is your issue even on their radar? If not, how can you get it onto their radar? What do they care about more generally, and how can you connect this issue to their major concerns?

Figure 11 shows that the CEO was viewed as the major authority figure for this challenge and values:

- financial outcomes
- customer satisfaction
- project outcomes.

The pizza also indicates from the way that it is shown that the executive team is all on-board with the same view as the CEO, and the board is too. That makes a pretty powerful faction that is closely aligned with the Project Team headed up by a relatively new IT Manager. The IT Manager's influence has been strong within this organisation and her reputation to deliver project goals within predetermined timelines is on the line. She is fiercely intelligent and single minded. A new project team, that is very loyal, has been formed around her.

Now proceed in a similar vein around your system of interest. Who are the key factions in play? When you have completed your pizza, ask: 'Who is missing?' It is easy to overlook an important faction because of our habitual ways of perceiving. Analysing the pizza in terms of factions will enable you to be more strategic and political in your approach.

The pattern of values is a way of understanding the politics

By political, I do not mean being self-serving in a Machiavellian manner. I hope your intention is to promote the health of the entire system or the greater good. By being political, I mean understanding what is of concern to people and working your issue through the system of people.

Many idealists believe that politics is not a game for them and that a good idea should stand on its own. Unfortunately, that is not how the world appears to work. If you want to make progress on your adaptive challenge, you need to be political in your approach. Taking a political approach may represent adaptive work for you. The politics can be viewed as no more or less than **understanding and engaging with the pattern of mental models or values in the system**.

Analyse the pattern of values, fears and loyalties in your pizza. Allies have a similar pattern of values to you. Working with allies reduces some of the hazards involved in leading adaptive or transformational changes. As extreme examples of the danger of adaptive leadership, think about the suffragettes who were jailed, Martin Luther King Jr., who was assassinated, or perhaps the person in your workplace who 'banged on' about one issue so long that everyone stopped listening.

Rather than being assassinated, in organisational contexts, the danger to avoid is being sidelined because people just don't want to think about your challenge. They naturally view it through a technical lens. These typical responses generate a common group dynamic to remove or sideline the person who is raising the adaptive challenge. This response may be conscious or not, and it is a part of a natural avoidance or denial mechanism. **Work avoidance**, as Heifetz, Grashow and Linsky (2009) call it, is very human. You can anticipate it and prepare for how you will deal with it when it arises.

The range of values in your pizza also begins to refine the scope and nature of the adaptive work that we discussed earlier. Reassess it again. What might be the adaptive work?

In the example in Figure 11, the analysis described above identifies two broad views in the system. These are summarised in Table 6. As you review the list of shared values and concerns, you can perhaps see a focus on 'deliverables' by one group and on 'involvement or process' by the other group. The adaptive work may be for each group to appreciate the other more. That is one hypothesis.

Table 6: Example factions and values from the example in Figure 11

Factions and their alignment	Shared values and concerns
• CEO, executive team and board • Project team • Provider	• Reputation, $s and project outcomes (deliverables)
• Us (the group in the room at the time) • Users	• User competence and confidence with the new system • On-board to use the system • Business as usual or minimal disruption (involvement or process)

What is the adaptive work or shift that you are trying to make progress on? Remember that it's just a hypothesis – you can't know what is right. You must experiment your way forward.

The pizza offers a limited view of the system

I believe that the pizza is a really useful analytical tool, but it alone doesn't tell all of the story – what could? The pizza works at the level of social patterns. And it brings an awareness of mental models (and values) through identifying the stories that people tell, and the fears they hold in relation to your issue.

The pizza is, however, silent on the direct and significant influence of the ruling paradigm that is institutionalised in different structures. These issues are taken for granted unless they are directly implicated by the adaptive issue being investigated. I am referring to structures such as the taken for granted hierarchy and its power constructs, organisational structure employing functional silos and job descriptions, performance review processes and so on. These elements of the organisational system are underpinned by mental models and influence people's behaviour. It's as though our adaptive analysis floats upon the surface of larger paradigmatic assumptions.

Systems thinkers such as Edwards W. Deming have long recognised that the system itself is responsible for 90–95% of the outcomes from the system (Scholtes 1988). The system comprises each individual, the processes and physical systems (e.g. information management systems and the IT hardware), and the culture of the organisation (which also integrates the broader community's culture). This is indeed a complex system.

The pizza is also silent on the behaviour of the system over time, it is an analysis at a point in time.

The iceberg model – offering more perspectives

To prompt a deeper or broader observation and interpretation of your adaptive issue within the structure of the system, we can employ the **iceberg model** (Figure 12) from the discipline of systems thinking. This model is intended to help us realise that there are different levels of observation and intervention in the system and that these levels, or ways of seeing, are associated with increasing degrees of leverage.

Figure 12 identifies five different levels, rather than the usual four, because I have added the vision, and therefore purpose, of the system (Kim 1996).

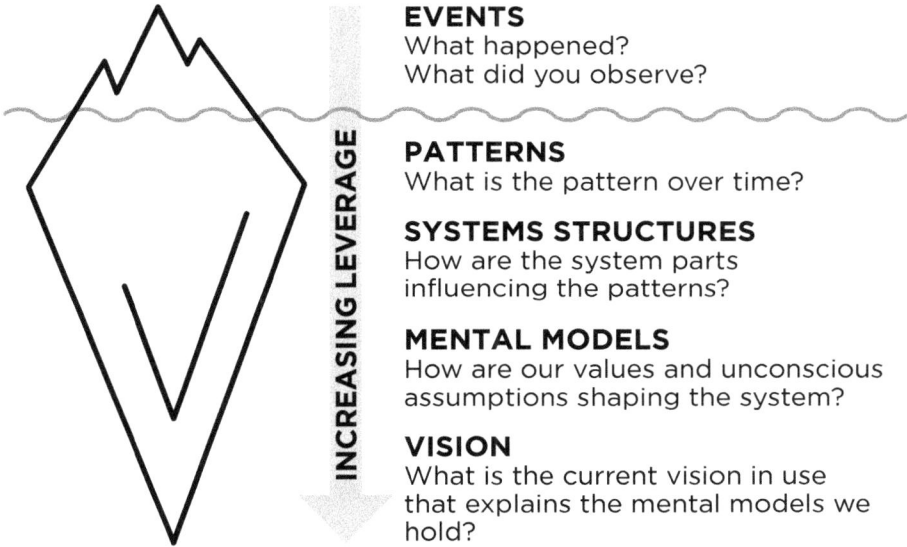

EVENTS
What happened?
What did you observe?

PATTERNS
What is the pattern over time?

SYSTEMS STRUCTURES
How are the system parts influencing the patterns?

MENTAL MODELS
How are our values and unconscious assumptions shaping the system?

VISION
What is the current vision in use that explains the mental models we hold?

INCREASING LEVERAGE

Figure 12: Iceberg model (adapted from Sweeny and Meadows, 1995, p243)

The levels and questions that you might inquire into at each level are described as follows. (The questions I employ below are drawn from Daniel Kim's (1996) work.)

1. **Events:** This level captures the stories about what is happening within the system and the events that have been observed that indicate there is an issue. The question you might ask is 'What have we observed that indicates we have a problem?'

2. **Patterns:** This level of observation adds the dimension of time. Ask: 'What is the pattern of events over time?' As you explore this question in a group, consider if the stories that emerge support the proposition that there is indeed a pattern over time. If you are considering a quality issue regarding a service or product, you might also add consideration of whether the event you are observing is merely an expression of natural variation, or not.

3. **Systems structures:** At this level we are concerned with structures within the system that may be producing the pattern of events. Ask: 'Which specific structures are producing the pattern of events?' and 'Which structures are the dominant influence?'

4. **Mental models:** Here we want to identify the mental models from which the systemic structures in level 3 are derived. Ask: 'What mental models do we hold that mean such structures were generated?' and 'What mental models maintain those structures?'

5. **Vision:** At the deepest level in the system is the vision or paradigm from which the mental models arise. Sometimes this is articulated, but often it is not. In considering the system as it currently is (rather than your desired vision articulated in Element 1), ask questions such as 'What kind of vision are we operating out of that explains the mental models we hold?' or 'What is the current vision in use?'

An example of a systemic, adaptive response to an event

1. Seeing at the level of event

The context is that of a meeting with an executive team reflecting on how to deal with the resignation of their colleague just the previous day. Their colleague was stressed and under-performing when she left. I spoke with her the day before and she indicated that she was disappointed and surprised by the way she was behaving. She described being quite short with people and feeling quite defensive. In conversation with the team on this day, they confirmed these self-observations, although their colleague was no longer with them. The executive team felt a bit embarrassed about not being able to hold people in her position. 'How do we keep picking the wrong person?' was one of the first questions that emerged from the meeting.

2. Seeing at the level of pattern

The resignation in question was the third in three years from this particular role. During the flurry of thinking about how to manage the missing director's function while recruiting another incumbent, it can be easy to forget asking: 'Is this more than coincidence? What structures within the organisation are producing this unintended result?' When faced with these questions, the team started reflecting on how all three incumbents had displayed similar patterns of behaviour before resigning. They had become more withdrawn from the rest of the team and defensive when peers had inquired and tried to help. The conversation also confirmed that they were trying to be genuinely helpful to their colleague.

3. Seeing the level of structure

I asked them to put the idea that there was something wrong with the incumbent aside for a moment and consider what structures in the organisation may have caused these outcomes. The team found a pattern that exists in the timing of annual projects and tasks. They spent some time discussing how the distance between functional departments seems to grow at certain times of the year. They started identifying how they could influence that flow of work to produce different outcomes. They also began to identify how the role of director of the department in question could be distributed over different departments to produce a better fit with the workflow.

What else may contribute to an increasing sense of stress for people in this role? The team identified structures including communication patterns that emerged from specific meetings. Additionally, they identified the inconsistent usage of specific communication and project management platforms. They determined to model and 'champion' the use of these in stand-up meetings.

4. Seeing at the level of mental models

'How might the capacity of others influence the role in question?' The team was really starting to think more broadly by the time this question arose, and they identified mental models that influenced lack of team management skills – this was now a broader issue than merely the event that triggered the meeting. The mental model was that there was not time in their fast-paced and seasonal business to develop younger managers. The lack of capacity has resulted in senior managers working longer hours and feeling more stressed. It also means that the organisation is more vulnerable to the departures of key people. The conversation moved into organisational culture, training and succession.

5. Seeing at the level of vision

Our conversation that day commenced with a process of recollecting the vision we had previously generated for the way in which the team would operate and the intention or goals we held for the current conversation. The entire conversation was undertaken within that context, and we drew connections to these elements.

Resulting from these insights, the team has decided not to recruit for this specific role again. They organised another meeting to redesign the role, splitting it into two different existing positions that sit in different parts of the organisation. They are disrupting the structures from which the behaviours emerge. These structures are both organisational structures and the thinking patterns within the executive team. They anticipate that this redesign will change the system that produced the stress and patterns that resulted in good people resigning.

If I had to sum up the adaptive shift in this conversation described above, I would say it was from a technical or single-loop solution – perceiving the problem as the person in the role – to perceiving more systemically – perceiving the influence of the organisational system on the role and the person in the role. The questions provided a systemic scaffolding for the conversation.

Element 4: Best guesses about the adaptive work

The case study above also provides a small insight into identifying the adaptive work that is the ultimate interpretation of the system. That identification can be seemingly quite difficult, perhaps because the process is conceptual and ambiguous. There is no scientific formula. It begins with observing behaviour, listening carefully to what is being said and by whom, and interpreting or making intelligent guesses! The interpretation shifts from a technical 'I know the answer' perspective to a systemic perspective that runs contrary to the ruling norms or ways of doing things.

I imagine the adaptive work as a shift from a way of thinking and/or valuing to a new way of thinking and/or valuing. The idea of a shift is linear, but useful. Sometimes the shift looks like the inclusion of more than one value (as in the example in Figure 11 and Table 6).

Let me provide another example. Within organisations today, many executives want their organisations to be more collaborative to deliver better performance. Depending upon the specific organisation and its history and current state, the adaptive work might be thought of as a shift like the one detailed in Table 7. Included are two hypotheses about the adaptive work. Table 7 also illustrates the relationship between the mental models and values.

Table 7: Examples of identifying hypotheses of adaptive work or shifts

	From ➡	To
Hypothesis 1 Mental model	We can work on this issue on a functional basis and bring our individual solutions together at the end.	We have to solve this together to get all the perspectives on the table and generate synergy.
Valuing	Independence and efficiency.	Interdependency and effectiveness.
Hypothesis 2 Mental model	Collaboration means asking what people think and then the executive team making the best decision.	Collaboration means engaging everyone in sharing perspectives and then collectively making a decision.
Valuing	Authority and control.	Egalitarianism and broad participation.

Please don't see this example and think it's the solution to your problems. These two options are just hypotheses that we can test with an experimental intervention.

Observing is often intervening

Due to the deep socialisation of the Newtonian paradigm, we believe that we can observe a phenomenon without influencing what we are observing. Within living systems, this is not the case. When people are being observed, it is not uncommon for their behaviour to change because of the observation. Be aware that your observation may be an intervention in itself.

Secondly, the tools and frameworks provided in this chapter are to guide you to analyse your challenge and the system. I encourage you to use these processes within a team or group. As discussions are catalysed with people in your group, you are more clearly intervening within the system because you are all a part of that system. The discussion directs people's attention with questions and conversation that will broaden their perspectives and perhaps even encourage the occasional 'ah-ha' moment as they have an insight into why things are the way they are. Those people in your group may now have conversations that are different to ones they might have had before. That's when and how unplanned adaptation begins to emerge. So be thoughtful about who you begin this process with and how you begin – living systems are sensitive to starting points.

As we move into discussion about how to intervene more deliberately on a wider scale, remember that your analysis to date is not about finding the answer, but rather to develop hypotheses about how to influence the system. You need to run an experiment or two to determine if you are on track and to influence more broadly.

Reflection questions

1. To what degree do you already spend time seeking to understand the system before launching into action?

    _____

    _____

    _____

    _____

    _____

    _____

2. How attached are you to your own interpretations and answers or solutions?

    _____

    _____

    _____

    _____

    _____

3. How could you involve more people as you seek to understand more about the system of interest?

    _____

    _____

    _____

    _____

    _____

CHAPTER 8

How to get into the action

When considering how to take action, we need to remember that the purpose is to learn more about the system and how to influence it. The emphasis is on learning.

Each iterative step forward is a process of learning together where a feature is that everyone learns something different. So, if you are operating in a group, it's important to gather together and reflect on what is being learned.

Another feature of intervening in the system is that it can occur in many different ways concurrently.

In the following section I will describe a formal, planned group process and more informal approaches. These are not steps identified in order to lead you to the solution. The approaches are not in any order of effectiveness. Instead, they are approaches that you might consider as you prepare to take action to liberate learning and change.

Element 5: Designing an experiment

Having completed the pizza exercise, you will be able to identify patterns in the values within the system. These patterns will help you to discern where to intervene and how.

Conceptually, the aim of designing an intervention is to decide how to act politically and strategically to be most effective in influencing the adaptation within the system. Your experiments may be individual conversations or extensive group processes. The choice between these approaches depends upon the context.

To understand how to decide how and where to intervene, let's return to the example that we explored in Element 3 (Figure 11 and Table 6) and imagine that you are leading this intervention. At least two ways forward are evident.

One pathway may be to discuss the adaptive issue – 'learning to deliver system changes' – with the CEO first, and then decide the next step after that conversation. The desired outcome of this conversation from the intervener's perspective may be two-fold. Firstly, to confirm (or not) the initial assessment of what the CEO values most about this issue. Secondly, gaining her support for a broader conversation with other factions to consider: 'What are we learning about delivering technology projects in a way that supports stronger business results and end users uptake?' You may notice that the broader conversation is framed differently now to reflect the values that we think may reach across and engage both major factions.

Facilitation of the larger and more formal process needs to enable multiple perspectives to be shared. The sharing and learning from each other may provoke positive adaptations by all present at the meeting. The type of facilitative process also needs consideration. The broad choice is between a meeting with a formal structure and one that is facilitated with little more than a central question. More structured methods can carry quite a lot of the load of enabling adaptive learning. The less formal approach relies more heavily on the skill of the person leading the discussion – or exercising leadership. In Chapter 9, I identify appropriately structured processes that may assist you, in addition to discussing how to facilitate an informal process.

As you design your intervention, think carefully about how an environment for open and honest sharing can be nurtured. Especially consider the politics and power of authority figures and how the process includes them in a way that does not compromise honesty from everyone. Cultivating openness may include preparing the CEO and executive team upfront.

For some organisational interventions, I have even run workshops to prepare the authority figures, helping them decide the nature of their role and appropriate behaviour depending on the outcomes that they desire. Less intensive considerations may be as simple as thinking about who sits where during the gathering and how any small group discussions are fed back to the larger group. Typically, I would not ask authority figures to do this.

A second possible pathway may involve the IT manager earlier. Although not a key authority figure, the IT manager's participation is key. Within the context we have been discussing, another individual conversation may be helpful to gain commitment to the process. After all, this person has a lot to lose and seemingly little to gain, given our assessment of her current mindset. Should this one-on-one conversation occur before or after that with the CEO? It may be wise to do this after you have gained the CEO's commitment – or it may be the case that the CEO's support will not be forthcoming without that of the IT manager.

The conversation with the IT manager could be more complicated than the one with the CEO, because the very issue being raised questions the IT manager's competence. Not directly, but indirectly. Therefore, it is strategic and political to spend time developing a degree of trust and relationship with the IT manager. Alternatively, maybe an ally who already has that relationship with the IT manager could hold the conversation. Couch this conversation in terms of what is valued by the IT manager – the pizza indicates that this is 'reputation'. The aim is not to change this perspective, but merely to gain agreement to participate in the meeting(s) and genuinely listen to others' experiences.

I hope that you can see that there is no right answer to how to design an intervention. From my experience within organisations, I believe that the major success factor is understanding the politics and being sensitive to the needs of authority figures, while also telling the truth about what people are experiencing.

Framing conversations

Whether the adaptive conversation is with an individual or a group, you will want and need to consider how to frame the process. This is where you need to speak to the values involved and collect everyone together with what politicians refer to as the **moral high ground**, or what I refer to as the health of the whole system. An example of this is the large group topic emerging from the conversation with the CEO in the discussion above – that is, 'What are we learning about delivering technology projects in a way that supports stronger business results?' Stronger business results is assumed to be an outcome that everyone in this particular organisation can get behind.

Being strategic and political

I wonder what you are thinking and how you are feeling about the process I have described above. Some people tell me they believe the process of connecting into the values of others, as I have described, is **manipulative**. I can understand this perspective; however, I believe that the intention held for intervening in the system is paramount in deciding if an intervention is manipulative or strategic.

Your intention is something that other people can't see; they see your behaviours or actions. Your purpose, however, can often be sensed by others. No doubt, you have had experiences where you are talking with someone, and you begin to feel the hairs on the back of your neck bristle. You feel disturbed. You sense that you are being manipulated. Typically, you will not generate this feeling in others if you intend to obtain an outcome that is genuinely for the greater good – people will trust you because you are listening to them.

People are more likely to feel suspicious if you appear to be seeking a specific and self-serving outcome. I find myself circling back to Chapter 5, which focused on the notion of letting go of control. Do not push for a specific outcome – **your role is to bring the system together so that it can connect with itself**, hear itself, and learn from itself. With some helpful facilitation, the participants will identify an experiment that may help them and the system to adapt – your purpose is for the greater good or the improved health of the whole system.

Element 6: Implement your experimental intervention

Having designed your intervention or experiment, then the next element involves implementation. A major element in execution is managing the degree of discomfort that results in the conversations. Sometimes this discomfort is very evident as people's voices are raised in disagreement or moments of passionate storytelling. Sometimes, the discomfort is internal as participants become aware that their previously held view is not serving them and the whole organisation very well.

The degree of discomfort will vary depending upon:

- the issue and the pattern of values in the system

- people's willingness and ability to share their perspectives (this can be adaptive work in itself within many organisations)

- the power dynamics in the organisation.

As the degree of discomfort that accompanies these conversations rises, so too must your ability to **hold the space**. This term refers to your capacity to persist despite the initial and instinctual responses from other people that there is no problem (denial) and your rising feelings of discomfort. After this initial response, you need to continue to interpret what is happening and keep nudging the conversation into the more challenging adaptive (or double-loop learning) space. You must not allow a short circuit to reduce discomfort to emerge. This might typically manifest as the group insisting that authority figures fix the issue or allow the group to rush to a technical interpretation and solution. Other typical comfort-inducing solutions may include assigning a committee to investigate and return with recommendations. This type of process does not enable adaptive work on a broad scale.

Continue to nudge the group towards adaptation using a combination of statements and questions such as 'I understand that is your perspective and I wonder if, for the greater good of the business outcomes for the whole organisation, it would be wise to hear other people's perspectives too?' or 'From what has been shared so far, it sounds as though there are two different perspectives on this issue.' Then relate the two perspectives as even-handedly as you can for the group to consider.

On those few occasions when quite a lot of emotion, discomfort and heat may be generated, you may well have to employ some heat-dampening strategies such as:

- providing additional structure to the meeting (e.g. more obvious facilitation processes or PowerPoint presentations to guide the discussion)

- providing a stronger and clearer agenda

- pacing the work over a longer time frame and managing expectations from one meeting to the next

- employing some humour and allowing the conversation to wander off track for a little while

- naming the emotion and reason for it (i.e. the topic is obviously important to us all)

- calling a short break before returning to the discussion.

Speaking to values

The Australian education system, to the best of my knowledge, does not teach oration at school. As a result, very few people are skilled in public speaking to influence. However, if you want to sway people's views and speak in a way that enables people to consider the adaptive work, then **speak to the values** that are in play in the issue you have identified. And speak in a way that unites rather than divides people.

Also, use the power of stories, and embed the values in those stories. Stories hold the complexity of both your adaptive issue and the complexity of humanity. Choose a personal story that is relevant to the issue – it will engage people emotionally (because it connects to their memories).

If we wanted to influence an adaptive issue through a story rather than a facilitated process, we might think about it in the following way.

- The presentation might begin with a personal recollection about the most recent system delivery and different people's experiences of it.

- We could name or identify the concerns that underpinned different factions within the story.

- Then we could share a story of how we think everyone could experience the benefits if the adaptive issue was successfully addressed. This would tell the story of the co-created vision from Element 1. It is a rich story that embeds the values of the post-adaptation state. This story provides a new possibility for people. Tell it in a way that encourages people to imagine themselves in that new state or way of doing things.

- Ideally, if possible, close by asking people to discuss what they think about the vision story and ask how they think it might be achieved. This conversation is the personal meaning-making that encourages further adaptive work for each individual.

- However, if like Martin Luther King in his 'I Have a Dream' speech we are speaking to thousands, we may have to close with a call to action. We could suggest an experiment that people could try out to see what would happen. Stress that they don't have to commit to it for all time. It's just an experiment.

Experiments are brilliant because if they are successful, people will perpetuate the experimental action because of the positive reinforcement loop that is created for each person.

Informally seeding ideas

Another less formal way of working with emergent change is to sow seeds of change. These are new ideas that are floated within the social ecology of the organisation. You may do this very deliberately or quite unconsciously. Let me provide two examples.

A couple of years ago, I was facilitating a group of people in a leadership development program. They had endured a rough time through changes in the administration of the program. The group's feelings of anger and frustration often turned into a critical view of any speaker's perspective, and the group members frequently asked questions that pulled the speaker down, rather than creating a space to learn from them. I wanted to raise this issue, but there was a complicating issue. It was politically difficult for me to do this because the group's frustration with the administration was often directed at me. Listening to me posit the idea that they were being negative was probably not going to be very influential. Instead, I chose to seed my observation with several people with high degrees of influence in the group. In casual conversations I asked how well they thought the group was managing to learn from speakers. (I was using the value of learning as a reflection of the health of the whole or the high moral ground mentioned earlier.) As we spoke, I offered my view that perhaps the group might benefit from shifting its perspective of guest speakers from being critical to being open to learning from the speaker. It was later that evening that I began to observe different types of questions being posed. The attitude shift spread to most within the group, but not all, over the following month.

As another example, I am part of a small group of people who have chosen to meet regularly and chew the fat together over lunch for two hours every month or so. The purpose is to hear what each of us is doing in our quite different areas of work and support each other to open up new lines of thinking and new possibilities that we are unable to perceive on our own. This group is a powerful incubator for novel ideas, new learning, and subsequent change. It is easy to underestimate the power of conversations like these because we often do not witness the outcomes – the effect is non-linear and indirect. The results of these new conversations are seeds that grow over time – and of course, not all seeds grow.

Seeds can lay dormant for varying amounts of time, waiting for suitable conditions before shooting above the soil and into the air. If it's a long time before the seed emerges, then it may pop up in a place where you never see it at all. Some seeds die. And when the ideas seeded within your conversations do emerge, rarely do they emerge with a hashtag on them that attributes them to you!

Lack of attribution circles back to the earlier identification of one of the qualities of the leader as gardener – **humility.**

A personal quality for seeding ideas is that of being willing to accept that you will usually gain no recognition for your input. But it was never your idea; humans are such social beings, and our thinking is very social. Your ideas develop because you have heard or read other people's opinions. Leadership through seeding ideas is selfless and focuses on the greater good.

Self awareness within the system

As you implement your intervention in the system, two important factors will influence how successful you are in your quest to influence others. These factors are how others perceive you and how well you adapt. Both of these factors are necessary because you are a part of the system – not separate from it.

As you implement your experimental intervention, your attention needs to be inwards on how you are feeling – it's part of the information you are gathering, and of course you need to regulate your responses too. But your attention also needs to go outwards. Keep observing yourself and others to gather data about how you are being seen. Are you influencing? Who is being influential, and why? How can you be more influential?

Observing like this is a challenging exercise – it requires you to be in the action and like a fly on the wall at the same time. If you can't do both at the same time, then practise alternating positions.

The story I shared earlier about seeding an idea within the leadership program group is also an example of observing how to be most influential within that context. I was aware that intervening directly to help participants to get out of their own way of achieving a major goal of the program was not going to work because of how they perceived me. A more indirect pathway that involved people they admired and trusted within the group was more likely to be successful. It was a more subtle form of intervention.

Be prepared to alter your views and be a continuous learner. Allow other people's ideas to permeate your mind and heart to adapt your understanding and thoughts.

Reflection questions

1. How are you being perceived?

   _____

   _____

   _____

2. How well is that perception helping you achieve your purpose?

   _____

   _____

   _____

3. How do you need to be perceived?

   _____

   _____

   _____

4. Who could you work with, and in what manner to increase your influencing capacity?

   _____

   _____

   _____

5. How could you raise your profile to be more influential within the relevant systems?

   _____

   _____

   _____

CHAPTER 9

How to monitor your progress

A major concern for many people when first entering the world of complexity is how to answer the question 'How will we know if we are making progress?' We are so deeply conditioned to the Newtonian notion of setting Specific, Measurable, Attainable (or Ambitious), Realistic, and Tangible (SMART) goals, that we assume that goal achievement is the only way to monitor our progress.

This chapter explores how deeply organisations are enthralled by goals, measurement and quantitative data, and some limitations of this SMART approach. We are exploring this topic because I want to persuade you to alter your practices to what many may consider a management heresy – to employ qualitative and subjective data to help you determine if your change process if making progress. We will begin by considering your decision making in your private life, and later in this chapter I will describe how to generate and use qualitative data in conjunction with your co-created vision.

Decision making in the complexity of life

Stop and consider your personal life for a moment. I guarantee you have made decisions **without knowing** what the outcome will be. For example, you went on a romantic date, maybe you went on holidays together, then you may have decided to take the leap and enter into marriage and then maybe even have children. All of these decisions were made without knowing the end point or outcome.

Life is the ultimate experience of complexity. You are an expression of complexity within a system brought to life through its untraceable pathways of relationships of interdependence. Although we often describe life as a journey – it's not. You are not headed to a predetermined destination (other than the ultimate finalisation of your own life force). It is a life, and, as Alan Watts suggests, a better metaphor for your life may be that of a dance. Life is a dance, where your task at any time is to decide what type of dance you will dance.

As you engage in the dance of life, how do you know if the decisions that you have made at different points in your life are serving you well or not? I believe that your (probably largely unconscious) process may be like this. You:

1. Spend time thinking about what you really want – generating a story about this future state and what it might be like if all were to go well.

2. Determine how you feel about the different options – weighing up the pros and cons.

3. Try an option out – you experiment.

4. Assess how well the lived experience matches your aspirations and dreams – your vision. You adjust accordingly.

We can employ a similar process to assess how the adaptive change process within our organisations is progressing too. To do this, measures will not always be appropriate, and indicators will be required. But this thinking goes against what is considered common sense within organisations today.

Debunking the myth: 'If you can't measure it, you can't manage it'

Why are we so hell-bent on measuring and objectifying?

As previously discussed, our organisations have been strongly influenced by the Newtonian paradigm. And the received management wisdom is a subset of this paradigm. It includes ideas encapsulated by a famous misquote that is often attributed to W. Edwards Deming: 'If you can't measure it, you can't manage it.'

In fact, Deming never said this, and more importantly, never meant this! As explained by The Deming Institute, the quotation has been taken out of context (Hunter 2015). The actual quotation is '*It is wrong to suppose that if you can't measure it, you can't manage it.*' Deming was very passionate about evidence-based decision making and encouraged people to use data. He was also aware that there are two types of data – quantitative and qualitative. Let's challenge the assumption that quantitative data is better than qualitative data – it depends upon context and purpose.

Quantitative data is not wrong, or bad. That is not the message I want to leave you with, but I do encourage you to question assumptions about:

- quantitative data being superior for management purposes
- being able to measure without affecting what we are measuring.

Can we measure without affecting the system?

It is also worth spending time considering how data collection itself and measurement feedback might influence the system. Is your measurement methodology generating a self-fulfilling prophecy?

Immersed as we have been within the Newtonian paradigm for so long, we have been deeply conditioned to believe that our observation of a specific item has no effect on the system we are observing. But think again. A system will deliver what it is designed to deliver.

As an example, let me relate a measurement process that I come across quite frequently in my cultural evolution work.

It is not uncommon for executive teams to want to understand if their investment in developing people to behave in more constructive ways is actually translating into a better culture. To identify progress, staff are asked to participate in a culture survey, and measurements are made team by team. If a team's survey results indicate that their culture is not quite as it could be, the team is invited to take part in further workshops to discuss their current culture results and make plans for further progress to be made. ('Invited' is an interesting word to use in this context. Sometimes it is a genuine invitation, but a genuine invitation can be declined. I wonder how many staff members feel they can refuse the invitation.)

The process of making new plans is always made as constructive as possible; however, the major point is this: in systems terms, the process of extra workshops (taking time and emotional effort) for those teams that deliver survey results that are less than desirable may be viewed as a type of punishment. The opposite is also true –those teams that deliver cultural survey results that are perceived as positive are rewarded with less workshops and less difficult conversations. It doesn't take the teams long to work out how to respond and deliver a positive assessment. Can you see how this process, designed with the best of intentions, can lead to false measurements and unintended consequences? The **measuring and feedback process is influencing the system** in an unhelpful manner. It is a graphic example of how we need to take extreme care when we choose what to measure and how.

An aside about culture

Given my understanding of culture, I am still not convinced that culture can be measured. Schein (1990) describes culture as:

> a pattern of basic assumptions, invented, discovered or developed by a given group as it learns to cope with its problems of external adaptation and internal integration that has worked well enough to be considered valid and, therefore is to be taught to new members as the

> *correct way to perceive, think and feel in relation to those*
> *problems.*   (Schein 1990, p. 111)

How can we measure that pattern of assumptions? The surrogate is behaviour, because it seems observable and measurable. However, observing a behaviour does not help us understand why that organisation or group of people believe such behaviour is appropriate. Behaviour is an artefact of culture – not the culture. Culture is an emergent outcome of the complexity of each organisation – its history, physical location, people, society in which it is embedded, and its purpose.

Distinguishing measures and indictors

Measures or quantitative data is reductionist data about a specific part of the system. This means that while it might reflect concrete facts about the system, we need to exercise care about the meaning we attribute to the data as we interpret its meaning. All too often we think we are not adding meaning as we report facts, but it is inevitable. Humans are interpretative or meaning-making organisms.

Qualitative data is contextualised data that is helpful in understanding and making meaning of complexity. Qualitative data, a story, is capable of relating complexity. A disadvantage of qualitative data, or one person's account, is that it is often not able to be generalised to gain a sense of how prevalent an issue is in the broader system. Qualitative data can be made more responsible and less subject to one person's perspective by discussing its meaning in a group of people from the system of interest. We gain a systemic sense of the qualitative data – as displayed in the example of employing the iceberg model in Chapter 7. Discussions about indicators are often employed to gain a sense of the health of the whole in complex systems, and these indicators are usually, but not always, qualitative.

The data we use most often to make decisions in our society is deliberately de-contextualised data in an effort to make it objective. Reductionist data focuses attention on one specific part of the system. For example, Gross national product (GNP) is one figure about how much an economy produces. But it has come to be understood, and promoted by politicians, as an indicator of how well society is doing. So, putting the purist economics understanding to one side for a moment, consider the following quotation from presidential candidate Robert F. Kennedy (1968):

> *Gross National Product counts air pollution and cigarette advertising, and ambulances to clear our highways of carnage. It counts special locks for our doors and the jails for the people who break them. It counts the destruction of the redwood and the loss of our natural wonder in chaotic sprawl. It counts napalm and counts nuclear warheads and armoured cars for the police to fight the riots in our cities. It counts Whitman's rifle and Speck's knife, and the television programs which glorify violence in order to sell toys to our children. Yet the gross national product does not allow for the health of our children, the quality of their education or the joy of their play. It does not include the beauty of our poetry or the strength of our marriages, the intelligence of our public debate or the integrity of our public officials. It measures neither our wit nor our courage, neither our wisdom nor our learning, neither our compassion nor our devotion to our country, it measures everything in short, except that which makes life worthwhile. And it can tell us everything about America except why we are proud that we are Americans.*

The pattern that I notice is how often we use reductionist data to attempt to decide what to do when we hope to intervene in larger complex systems. Reductionist, quantitative data will not, on its own, help to us to resolve complex challenges. We need to be aware of reductionism even down to the habits of what we count as data and what we take notice of as we try to decide what to do.

Table 8 summarises the differences between measures and indictors. The table itself is generalised, because it is possible to find measures that reflect the health of the whole. For example, counting the number of species and individual frogs in a pond could provide a reflection of the health of the pond. This measure could be a good indicator. Similarly, in a recent conversation with a group of people concerned with improving communication and relationships within a university department, we discussed the possibility of monitoring the number of emails with carbon copies (CCs) to multiple recipients as an indicator of the state of communications and relationships. The assumption underpinning this measure is that if the number of emails with blanket CCs reduces, it may be a reflection of staff knowing rather than guessing who needs the information in the email. This may in turn be a reflection of knowing each other better, and maybe even talking with each other as a first option.

Measures are, by their nature, about things that have occurred in the past. They generally provide a rear-view mirror image of what has happened. Some indicators can be found that are leading or in advance of what is yet to occur.

Table 8: Measures contrasted with indicators

Measures	Indicators
Quantitative (usually)	Qualitative (usually)
Reductionistic	Holistic
Usually measures a part of a system	Reflects the health of the whole system
Lag – rear-view mirror	Leading

Indicators of success exist for your adaptation process

There may be measures that you can use to determine the success of your change process, but I suggest that caution should be exercised as you choose these – don't go with your first, common sense (fits with the ruling paradigm) idea. There are certainly indicators of the health of the whole that your group can develop from your co-created vision. These indictors will aid your deliberations about what changes your experimental interventions have generated, what you are learning and how successful you are to date. Deliberation in groups is a must – you have only one perspective. The following section identifies how to generate the indicators and assess them.

Element 7: Monitor your progress and repeat

The co-created vision, if you recall, fulfils at least four functions, the last of which was to provide a story that can be revisited for orientation when ambiguity is high, and motivation when energy inevitably wanes. We can also use the vision to monitor progress. We can observe whether the values embedded in the vision are being expressed more often or in a way that is a more satisfying expression of the value. Gather a group of people from within your system of interest and ask them to consider if they are seeing the values expressed more often and more fully than before your intervention.

An additional step if you wish is to also gather data from the system around you to support that conversation. The data may be qualitative or quantitative – remember to take care with how you collect this data.

One additional process that I sometimes employ is to generate indicators of success to help the group to identify the types of indicators that they might observe if their vision was coming into being.

Returning to the example we began working with in Chapter 7, Element 3, with the group of managers 'learning to deliver system changes', some indictors of success may be:

- users of new systems feel involved in systems changes
- users of new systems feel confident in the use of those systems
- substantive changes that benefit customers are evident.

In developing these indicators of success, I considered:

- the values that I hypothesise are at the heart of the adaptive challenge
- statements that can be discussed by a group over time to determine to what degree they are true
- a best guess of what might be observable if the organisation is adapting
- a small number of indictors – no more than five is ideal.

The indicators may need to be evolved over time as more is learned.

When my colleague Sam Wells and I wrote the original envisioning process (Wells & McLean 2013), we included developing indicators of success as a part of the process before taking action. Over time, however, we have realised that while we might do this, it is not necessary. Firstly, it seems to be a very adaptive conversation that can be difficult to facilitate in a large group. Secondly, identification of the indicators before experiments may in fact generate a temptation to treat the indicator like a goal. This is a perspective that may backfire. In the world of complexity, we remember that cause and effect is indirect and non-linear. An indicator is just that: an indicator – that is, an emergent outcome of a number of different dynamics and elements. Aiming action directly at it like we are used to doing to achieve a goal is unlikely to produce the intended result.

Reflection questions

1. What are you thinking and how do you feel about employing qualitative data to monitor progress of your change initiative?

_____

_____

_____

_____

_____

_____

2. Review a current measuring process, in what ways might the process is generating a self fulfilling prophecy or influencing the reported result?

_____

_____

_____

_____

_____

_____

CHAPTER 10

Practices that will help hone your skills

The skills required to exercise your leadership in systems to liberate the dormant potential for change have already been alluded to in the previous chapters as we explored:

- the principles underpinning the behaviour of living systems that form the lens through which you view the world
- the personal qualities and awareness that will serve you well
- the systemic analytical processes and tools that shape a framework for you to understand where and how to intervene in the system.

In this chapter I identify and discuss a few specific practices to help you to hone your skills. Practices are exactly that. You need to practise and develop specific skills and capacities. It takes time to learn and develop your level of awareness in a way that you can pick the difference between a Newtonian reaction and a systemic response within a living system context.

Practise personal reflection

Reflection is an important part of the process of becoming a more effective facilitator of change. Reflection develops the capacity to be reflexive, which is at the core of double- and triple-loop learning. Reflexivity is the ability to recognise how the way you interpret and see the world is influenced by your own biases, values and mental models. The way you see things influences what you do, so a reflexive stance means you recognise the way in which you might cause what has happened. A high degree of reflexivity will enable you to understand yourself more clearly in terms of your own norms, politics and desires. Reflexivity is therefore a pathway to authenticity. The type of reflection I am referring to here is one that goes beyond 'What happened?' but also asks and seeks to answer 'How did I contribute to that event occurring?' and then, 'If I was to do that again, what would I do differently?'

There are entire facilitative processes generated around the central idea of personal and group reflection and reflexivity – for example, action learning. Coaching is a process that highlights the importance of reflection. Some facilitation processes may focus on reflection as they guide groups to identifying what they have learned.

You will benefit from putting in place a process of personal reflection. For some people this takes the form of journaling. Some people run, some meditate, and some consider the day as they travel home after work. Find the process that works most effectively for you. The purpose of the reflection is to enable your own learning and development through increasing awareness of yourself and the system in which you are working.

Initially, you will find that you reflect at a distance from a specific event. With practice, your reflection will morph into awareness in the moment and become a part of the personal qualities that you are able to offer in service to others.

Practise noticing reductionism in all its subtle forms

Within your reflection process, focus some attention on how you are observing and interpreting events through the lens of living systems. Specifically, notice when you are drawn down the reductionist rabbit hole of the Newtonian paradigm. After 15 years of learning to observe differently, I still find myself noticing new nuances – new ways that the Newtonian habit of reductionism asserts itself.

Just the other day, for example, I noticed why I often feel so uncomfortable around some environmental activists despite being people I feel a great deal of kinship with. At the heart of our different approaches is the habit of reductionism. It is not uncommon for environmental activists to focus their attention on just one thing. When I explain why I think the approach of focusing on cultural change is more effective, some of these activists look at me in a slightly patronising manner that says: 'Yes, we understand – but it takes so long and is so difficult. We need to take direct action!' The problem with direct action, as they convey it, is that it most often ignores the complexity of contexts from which environmental issues emerge as a problem. The specific environmental issue is often not the real problem in itself. The source of the problem is elsewhere. It exists in the deeper patterns and habits of thinking that replicate themselves throughout our society in the way we approach economic development, agriculture, travel, technological development, education, religion – all of which combine to produce the environmental issue. Climate change is a classic example.

So, keep questioning yourself. Why do you think what you think?

Zooming in can retain the qualities of the whole

Appreciating the whole can be difficult because the whole is VERY big! If you take the logic of whole systems to its logical conclusion, you are seeking to understand the universe(s) as one system. So, at times we need to zoom in to a smaller part of the system – but this is not the same as reducing it to a part. This distinction has taken me years to gain!

As discussed in Chapter 7 in regard to Element 3, zooming in, by reducing the size of the system of interest, can be done in way that still keeps the nature and dynamic of the whole in view. Rather than focusing on one facet or part of the system, zoom in on a smaller geographical size – a microcosm of the whole. By doing this, all the complexity of the relationships within the whole should remain in the smaller holon.

Reductionism is the opposite of complexity

Reductionism is the opposite of appreciating the wholeness and inherent complexity of living systems. Some people think simplicity is the opposite of complexity, but simplicity exists within complexity. The opposite of complexity is our propensity to reduce things to parts – to slice and dice the whole. And this tendency can be very subtle and can be most evident in the type of data we employ to make decisions about where and when to intervene in systems. Be careful to use more than reductionistic quantitative data.

Practise noticing the tendency to apply reductionism in everything you do – develop your skill at noticing this in the moment and bringing that awareness to the groups you are working with.

Adaptive learning processes

Coaching – individually or in groups

My fascination to learn about emergent change was ignited by my experiences as an executive coach. I witnessed change happening every day. I saw it emerging as a result of the coaching conversations in which I was engaging with my clients. These are conversations that are characterised by:

- tapping into what the client wants to achieve (intrinsic motivation)
- asking rather than telling to raise awareness and a sense of responsibility to do things differently
- supporting the client to undertake their experiments to learn over time what may work for them.

Coaching is an approach that engages people in their thinking and weighing up of what to change and how. Coaching is an adaptive process.

The minor difference between pure coaching and the way in which you might employ coaching as an approach to exercise your leadership in adaptive challenges is that you do have an agenda – your purpose when exercising leadership for an adaptation. However, if your purpose is working for the health of the whole system and you remain open to your own adaptive work, it is unlikely that your purpose will get in the way of successful coaching.

Coaching is underpinned by two seemingly simple skills – listening and asking questions. Simple is not always easy though. Don't take these skills for granted. Practise them every day. If you haven't already, I recommend that you formally learn and then practise coaching skills.

Listening

Listening to the humanity of people, which often hides underneath what people say, is a highly developed communication skill. Listening for what people are really trying to say includes:

- quietening your own mind to give your full attention to the person you are engaging with

- remaining open to and curious about what they are saying

- noticing underlying emotions or concerns

- noticing the thinking patterns and assumptions that are becoming evident as the person speaks and as you notice your own reactions to what is being said

- noticing and integrating messages that are sent via body language, the language employed, the pace of the communication and the tone of communication

- listening for and respecting boundaries around the edges of stories people share

- hearing what this person really values, wants and needs.

How effectively do you listen? It may sound odd, but I find listening to orchestral music or jazz bands improvising to be very helpful in developing my listening skills. You may like to try practising your listening with your favourite music. Instead of listening to just the main melody, attempt to consciously hear each different thread of music of each instrument being integrated into the whole piece of music. You might begin by noticing the violins, then the trumpets, then the percussion, and so on. As you move on, don't lose the previous focus of attention, just add to it.

Develop a listening development plan for yourself – you might reflect on your progress at the end of each day.

Powerful questions

The second basic coaching skill is that of asking questions. There are no perfect questions, so don't bother with a list that you can use as a template. Instead, use your listening with openness and curiosity as your guide to determine what to ask about.

Peter Block (2018) identifies some useful qualities of powerful questions that you might practise. He suggests that powerful questions are:

- slightly uncomfortable or anxiety raising
- ambiguous
- personal.

For example: To what extent do you demonstrate your leadership responsibility more fully by learning to ask more powerful questions?

Again, I recommend reflecting on your practice in this regard.

Systems thinking questions

Within this topic of asking questions, there are a few questions that emerge from the practice of systems thinking that may help you – these are in addition to those identified in Chapter 7 when we identified the iceberg model and its layers as different ways of viewing a challenge. Questions from systems thinking are essentially focused on exploring the surrounding context to understand what may be influencing and how. For example, some questions inspired by systems thinking include (Bales 2009):

- What about our processes/systems is causing this to happen? What behaviour is being rewarded in this system and how? How might our organisational culture be influencing this outcome?

- Is the cause and effect relationship in this challenge difficult to notice because of the time separation involved? What unintended outcomes could eventuate if we implement this solution?

- How do we know that the challenge we are attempting to resolve is a symptom or a root cause of the problem?

- What solution might have the greatest influence? Where is the greatest leverage?

- What are the short-term pressures being felt by key people involved in this issue? What are the long-term consequences of this solution?

Facilitating emergence within larger conversations

I learned to facilitate groups by applying my coaching skills to large group conversations. Coaching is itself an emergent process of asking questions itself, so facilitating emergence in groups came very naturally to me. For a very long time, however, I felt that I had never really mastered facilitation because my processes were not as neat and tidy as those of other facilitators. I criticised myself for that without realising the difference between the processes and intent of each type of process.

A crucial difference for facilitation within the context of our current topic – liberating adaptation – is the purpose of the facilitation. There are many facilitation processes that are designed for different purposes, such as:

- planning

- gathering data about how people view specific topics to report back on

- decision making

- problem solving.

I am not talking specifically about any of these four areas of facilitation.

In our context of adaptive change, we are interested in facilitating group discussions that enable the system to hear itself, learn and adapt. By this I mean that the purpose of the facilitation is to enable the different perspectives to be heard by the different factions. Then, beyond hearing those different perspectives, to process them and use them to do personal and group or system-wide adaptive learning. From the learning and insights comes the possibility of doing things differently – or change as we have come to understand it.

We have already identified the need to develop the capacity to hold the space for this sometimes emotional work and let go of your own predetermined solutions and outcomes to enable emergence from the group. The topic of letting go of control has comes up continually within this book, because it can not be stressed enough.

Practise nurturing the conditions for emergence

Emergence is encouraged when the environment is lightly structured. So, consider increasing your own tolerance for the ambiguity that accompanies emergence. When you hold meetings:

- Don't set an agenda, except perhaps one central question of interest to all.

- Don't take official minutes. Everyone in attendance will have their own memory of the meeting and what was said. They have experienced it. Note-taking also adds an element of linear concreteness to the meeting that tends to limit the fluidity of conversations as they circle around.

- Encourage drawing ideas and concepts on a whiteboard to illustrate complex ideas.

- Encourage everyone to say exactly what they are thinking about the topic, and to practise saying it with respect and sensitivity towards others.

- Encourage listening. Everyone should practise listening to understand.

- Encourage curiosity. Everyone should practise questioning that digs deep with the purpose of uncovering mental models.

- Allow ample time. The clichéd quip that 'a good meeting is a short meeting' needs to be challenged. A good meeting is an engaging conversation where everyone participates.

Facilitative processes can carry a good deal of the load

My experience in both facilitating adaptive work within organisations and guiding change agents to learn how to facilitate adaptation has shown me that a great deal of the load can be borne by the facilitative process that you choose to employ. The facilitative process can hold a good deal of space for you. Some facilitators do not pre-plan any process other than turning up and opening a conversation around a desired outcome (notice the distinction between outcome and output). Others like to have a preselected process.

Table 9 highlights some of my favourite facilitative processes to use to create a container for adaptive work. By container, I mean a process for a specific group over time. Table 9 also indicates where you can gain detailed, free assistance online to learn when and how to use each process.

Table 9: Facilitative processes for adaptive work

Process	Online address to learn more
Open Space Technology	https://openspaceworld.org/wp2/open/
Appreciative Inquiry	https://appreciativeinquiry.champlain.edu/
World Cafe	http://www.theworldcafe.com/key-concepts-resources/world-cafe-method/
Envisioning	https://www.mdpi.com/2079-8954/1/4/66
Warm Data Labs	The only process that you need to be accredited to use (The International Bateson Institute). Learn more at https://batesoninstitute.org/warm-data-labs/

When choosing your process:

• Use your systemic analytical processes and tools to determine how you think you might best attract people, rather than compel people, to the discussion.

• Consider where you are in the adaptive process, where each meeting or conversation is just one part in a larger and indeterminant process.

• Make sure that the process empowers attendees and that the process itself is transparent and fair.

• Begin the discussion from where the attendees are – not where you are.

• Make sure that you are including and working across the different factions in the system.

• If people begin to identify ways in which they will lose something, then acknowledge that loss – and help them to move forward regardless.

• Encourage experimentation to learn.

Public speaking

It can never hurt to develop your capacity to be in the limelight and speak to larger audiences. Some say that speaking in public is feared more than death. I can't understand this, except that death may seem rather remote when you are young and healthy.

In the section about seeding ideas in Chapter 8, I described how you might speak to values. If you are intent on making a difference, then you need to be able to speak confidently and clearly in public. I encourage you to develop this skill and develop your capacity to speak to groups of people when you need to. Groups such as Toastmasters and Rostrum are highly supportive groups that also contain a solid structure to assist your development.

Reflection questions

1. How, when and where do you or will you practise regular reflection and develop your reflexive capacity?

    _____

    _____

    _____

2. Where can you try out some of the ideas presented here with a degree of safety? (The idea is to test the ideas and practices, not put yourself in harm's way as you are practising.)

    _____

    _____

    _____

3. What specific skills or knowledge do you most need to acquire now?

    _____

    _____

    _____

4. Who can help you hold yourself accountable for your own development?

    _____

    _____

    _____

CHAPTER 11

The hope, simplicity and power implicit in complexity

> *For the simplicity on this side of complexity, I wouldn't give you a fig. But for the simplicity on the other side of complexity, for that I would give you anything I have.*
>
> – Oliver Wendell Holmes

We have come to the end of this book about how to liberate emergent change. It is full of big little shifts – seemingly small shifts in the way we perceive challenges and respond to them that hold the possibility of very large shifts in outcomes.

You have exposed yourself to some new ideas and refreshed some ideas that are already familiar to you. Once you know something, you cannot un-know it. Once your mind has been stretched, your practice will help maintain the new shape. I do hope that you have begun to experiment with some of the new ideas.

The journey of Big Little Shifts

As you put these ideas into practice, you will integrate ideas as knowing. You will be travelling further along the path described in Chapter 2. It may be interesting to review that pathway again now. What has been your movement already? What are you noticing about your journey that may be similar or different to that which I have laid out?

My ambition has been to help you, through understanding more about perceiving the world through the lens of living systems, to seed adaptation within you, so that you might help others with a similar experience. This is what is meant by the term **inside-out change**.

You may recall that we spent some time clarifying terms such as change, adaptation and transformation in Chapter 3, where we linked these terms to single-, double- and triple-loop learning respectively. Learning is what living systems do to adapt. We also started to raise awareness around the pervasiveness of the Newtonian paradigm that we have all been immersed within in our western culture and our organisations. We began to explore the very different behaviour of living systems, or complex adaptive systems. Living systems continually pass information in various forms to each other through their interdependence – each sub-system learning from others and adapting when it makes sense.

Because perceiving through the lens of living systems is so important, we spent some time in Chapter 4 clarifying what that lens offers with regard to perspectives on what we might do to exercise our leadership for adaptation. The leadership principles related to how change emerges and also integrated the idea that because people are an expression of nature as living systems themselves, we can engage with the powerful natural forces within people to liberate the often dormant, yet powerful natural creativity, within everyone.

You read extensively in Chapter 5 about the need to be aware of the need for control – individual and organisational – and to let it go as much as is humanly possible. The shift from control to liberation of possibilities is crucial.

In Chapter 6 we identified the energetic shift to replace the desire for control with the desire to be someone who liberates possibilities within others. We briefly explored the metaphor of a leader as gardener rather than the more action-oriented and forceful hero – a leader with liberation at heart, rather than control. Importantly, we identified qualities such as humility, to foster within yourself.

As we moved from perception and being in the lower two bands of the Big Little Shift framework model (Figure 2), I recognised that the tools and frameworks in the remainder of the book are provided as a scaffold of types to help you integrate the perception and being. Once integrated, you may well find that you no longer require the content in Chapters 7 and 8. Nevertheless, these chapters are very important for now because they provide the tools of a new way of perceiving. They provide a language to describe what you are noticing.

If you attempt to employ the tools that emerged from the mechanistic paradigm within your understanding of complexity, you will not achieve the results or outcomes that are possible. You will limit yourself and others to playing at the edges of the Newtonian paradigm. That may seem like progress and feel somewhat satisfying. For example, I often hear people say that 'some change is better than no change'. But that is not necessarily the case! Some change (single-loop), might make you feel as though you have changed – and generate a false sense of progress. This can be a dangerous space to reside in. It can be a form of work avoidance or denial.

Chapter 9 identified different methods to monitor the progress of your adaptive or transformational initiative. We debunked the myth that 'if you can't measure it, you can't manage it' and found that this received wisdom is incorrect in expression and substance. The co-created vision from Chapter 6 re-appeared to guide us in determining if progress is occurring. The vision is a story of what is important – it embeds values. The values may be used to develop indicators of success – usually qualitative in nature. Progress on these indicators can be assessed by groups of people within the system of interest to agree on the degree of success and identify areas requiring attention. The process of discussing progress may also identify the need to evolve the vision based on what has been learned.

Chapter 10 provides recommended practices to help you hone the skills and behaviours associated with nurturing the workplace for adaptation. These are the skills and capacities of generating spaces in which emergence can be encouraged or nurtured. Emergence is a natural and always present potential of living systems. The structure of our organisations and the habits of management that have arisen from the mechanistic paradigm do not encourage emergence. The Newtonian paradigm favours control and the status quo.

Practising and staying in touch

The understanding of complexity and living systems may seem strange in comparison to more traditional management practices today, but it's much less strange today than it was 15 years ago. And it's much stranger today than it will be in another 5 years – our times are demanding that we understand how to work with complexity rather than dominate it.

This book shares some of what I have learned over 15 years of extensive research, learning and practice. It is not everything I have learned, and it does not include my current learning into whole systems change for a sustainable and flourishing future. I hope to share more about that in another book.

The next step for you, however, is to learn from doing.

Complexity offers hope and simplicity

Why am I so passionate about understanding and sharing how to facilitate adaptation and transformation in complexity? Because our world has so many pressing problems and complex challenges.

Daily we hear more news of the different systems in decline – education, health, childcare, agricultural, conservation, aged care and even economic systems. Major systems in our country and world are failing because they were designed for an age that has passed. A new era is being birthed.

As Gregory Bateson (1972) identified, it is the mismatch between the way we humans think the world works, and the way that nature actually works, that creates the major challenges that we now face.

Complexity offers a way of viewing these systemic challenges and a way of redesigning them – from inside our heads and hearts and out into the world. Some complexity practitioners are focused on modelling systems to find solutions to tell other people. The most important fault I find with this way of understanding complexity is that it tends to separate the people who are the problem from the problem. We are all a part of, or contributors to, that complexity and the adaptive issue. Further, living systems are inherently unpredictable – so an answer cannot be determined, although scenario analysis may be helpful.

Complexity offers us hope that organisations will begin to see their wellbeing as being interdependent with the health of the whole system, including the community and the natural environment. When organisations do recognise this, we should see the purpose of the organisation turn from being exploitive of people and the planet to caring for both people and the planet. It is the investigation into how this transformational and cultural shift may occur within organisations that has motivated me to research change and how it actually occurs.

Simplicity within complexity

I hope you have also started to recognise that although we have been exploring the complexity and interdependence of living systems, this approach offers simplicity.

Our approach employing the lens of living systems does not replicate the complicatedness of having to predetermine a path, and the stress of having to deliver that path. It avoids completely the sense of failure that many managers express when their plans do not come to fruition. It ignores the mechanistic assumptions about people being no more than their technical training. It restores balance to power and status differentials that have become a source of problems in themselves.

There is a simplicity in gathering people to ask and answer the question: 'How do you really want to experience this issue when it is resolved?' There is a simplicity in encouraging people to identify, work to and develop their strengths to encourage them to find new and innovative ways of working with complex challenges. There is simplicity in genuinely valuing everyone and listening to people rather than convincing them of solutions owned by others. There is simplicity, bravery and authenticity in working together in community rather than alone. There is simplicity in bringing different perspectives and ways of knowing together – to understand what we all do understand together. There is simplicity in experimenting your way forward to learn what works. There is simplicity and pragmatism at the heart of emergent change.

Powerful natural forces

Not only is there simplicity at the heart of complexity, but there is also power. Not the self-limiting power over people that some might desire. Rather, the power that is inherent in working with and influencing natural forces. So much more is possible when we learn that 'paddling together takes us further together' to quote a Māori proverb, Hoeangatahitia ki kō atu. And when we work together we can learn more about the powerful natural forces in which we are situated; the way in which the river is running and work with those forces too.

Complexity offers a new metaphor for leadership. By observing how nature organises itself, we are offered a different way of thinking about distributed leadership – one in which the collective moves as one, like starlings, creating magnificent and unpredictable patterns. A distributed leadership from anywhere within the organisation where people make decisions with reference to their understanding of the vision and values that are expressed purposefully.

We humans are a part of nature too. We are a force of nature with all its capacity for creativity and innovative experiments. We can trust in those powerful forces of nature.

Meeting complexity with complexity

All change begins as an imagining within us and manifests outside each one of us.

The impulse for change is not just the imagining or vision that you and others hold. The impulse for change is generated by the tension between the difference amid the current reality that you face and the possibility as described by your vision. The vision at the level of values expresses another way of being. Gregory Bateson discussed perception of differences and the ability to make distinctions as being at the heart of information that is significant. He described this as the *'difference that makes a difference'*. The difference between reality and vision is one of those differences that enables distinctions. Do not ignore the power that this difference can generate.

Once envisioned, adaptation and transformation do not usually manifest overnight. (Transformation rarely occurs because as holons within holacrhcy, we are connected to the larger whole. Transformation of one holon must take that interdependence into account. At the time of publication however, we have all just experienced a whole systems change in our context, making organisational transformation so much more possible.) It generally takes time and multiple iterations, learning as you experiment. What I learn will not be identical to what you learn, and we must learn together because doing so enables multiple perspectives and ways of knowing.

Being together enables us to better understand the complexity of challenges that we face. Being together is a source of complexity (and some frustration at times because of that complexity). We need multiple people and perspectives to create the emerging solutions we need to meet the complexity of the challenges that we face.

As much as we desire them, there are no silver bullet solutions to complex challenges.

Complexity must be met with complexity.

Epilogue

My curiosity and learning about complexity or living systems, leadership, and change continues unabated and you can remain in conact with me and my work through my websites. I currently have two; www.the-partnership.com.au and www.josiemclean.com.

I offer in-person and online programs and masterclasses in addition to speaking at conferences. You will also find a growing number of free videos to view in which I explain more about complexity.

Now that this book is complete, I intend to write another that shares what I have learned about partnering with organisations and people who are motivated to transform from exploiting our planet to nurturing it. This is a cultural shift which I believe is at the heart of humanity's response to the large threats including climate change and our collective (un)sustainability.

I look forward to remaining connected to you.

References

Argyris, C 2003, 'A life full of learning', *Organization Studies*, vol. 24, no. 7, 2003/09//, p. 1178+.

Argyris. Chris. *Overcoming Organizational Defenses*. 1990. Upper Saddle River, N. J.: Prentice-Hall.

Argyris, C. and Schön,D. (1978), Organizational learning: a theory of action perspective. New York, McGraw-Hill.

Amabile, TM 1997, 'Motivating creativity in organisations: on doing what you love and loving what you do', *California Management Review*, vol. 40, no. 1, Fall 1997, pp. 39–58.

Amabile, TM, Hadley, CN & Kramer, SJ 2002, 'Creativity under the gun', *Harvard Business Review*, vol. 80, no. 8, pp. 52–61.

Bales, B 2009, 'Systems thinking in practice', University of Texas, University, Austin.

Bateson, G 1972, *Steps to an ecology of mind*, 2nd edn, University of Chicago Press, Chicago and London.

Bateson, G 2002, *Mind and nature: a necessary unity*, 10th reprint edn, Hampton Press, Cresskill, New Jersey.

Beer, M & Nohria, N 2000, 'Cracking the code of change', *Harvard Business Review*, May–June 2000, pp. 133–141.

Block, P 2018, *Community: the structure of belonging*, 2nd edn, Berret-Koehler Publishers, Oakland, California.

Box, GEP 1979, 'Robustness in the strategy of scientific model building', in RL Launer & GN Wilkinson (eds), *Robustness in statistics*, Academic Press, Wisconsin.

Buckingham, M & Clifton, DO 2001, *Now discover your strengths*, The Free Press, New York.

Cook-Greuter, SR & Soulen, J 2007, 'The developmental perspective in integral counseling', *Counseling and Values*, vol. 51, no. 3, pp. 180–192.

Dunphy, D, Griffiths, A & Benn, S 2007, *Organizational change for corporate sustainability: a guide for leaders and change agents of the future*, 2nd edn, New York, Routledge.

Gumeracha Main Street, 2017, *Gumeracha main street project vision*, viewed 18 December 2019, <http://www.gumerachamainstreet.com.au/vision/>.

Heifetz, R, Grashow, A & Linsky, M 2009, *The practice of adaptive leadership: tools and tactics for changing your organisation and the world*, Harvard Business Press, Boston.

Heifetz, R & Linsky, M 2002, *Leadership on the line: staying alive through the dangers of leading*, Harvard Business School Press, Boston.

Higgs, M & Rowland, D 2005, 'All changes great and small: exploring approaches to change and its leadership', *Journal of Change Management*, vol. 5, pp. 121–151, DOI:10.1080/14697010500082902.

Hilborn, RC 2003, 'Seagulls, butterflies, and grasshoppers: A brief history of the butterfly effect in non-linear dynamics', *American Association of Physics Teachers,* vol 72 (4), DOI: 10.1119/1.1636492.

Hock, DW 1995, 'The chaordic organization: out of control and into order', *World Business Academy Perspectives*, vol. 9, no. 1, pp. 5–18.

Hock, DW 2005, *One from many: Visa and the rise of chaordic organization*, Kindle edn, Berrett-Koehler Publishers, San Francisco.

Hunter, J 2015, 'Myth: If you can't measure it, you can't manage it', blog post, *The W. Edwards Deming Institute Blog*, viewed 26 December 2019, <https://blog.deming.org/2015/08/myth-if-you-cant-measure-it-you-cant-manage-it/>.

Hutchens, D 1999, *Shadows of the Neanderthal: Illuminating the beliefs that limit our organizations*, Pagasus Communications, MA.

Kegan, R 1982, *The evolving self: problem and process in human development*, Harvard University Press, Cambridge.

Kennedy, RF 1968, *Remarks at the University of Kansas, March 18, 1968*, John F. Kennedy Presidential Library and Museum, viewed 29 December 2019, <https://www.jfklibrary.org/learn/about-jfk/the-kennedy-family/robert-f-kennedy/robert-f-kennedy-speeches/remarks-at-the-university-of-kansas-march-18-1968>.

Kim, DH 1996, 'From event thinking to systems thinking', *The Systems Thinker*, vol. 7, no. 4, p. 2.

Koestler, A 1976, *The ghost in the machine*, 2nd paperback edn, Picador, London.

Kotter, JP 2007, 'Leading change', *Harvard Business Review*, vol. 85, pp. 96–103.

Laloux, F 2014, *Reinventing organizations: A guide to creating organizations inspired by the next stage of human development*, 1st (revised) edn, Nelson Parker.

Maslow, A 1959, 'Creativity in self-actualizing people', in H Anderson (ed.), *Interdisciplinary symposia on creativity,* Harper & Row, New York, pp. 83–95.

Maturana, HR, Varela, FG & Uribe, R 1974, 'Autopoiesis: the characterization of living systems, its characterization and a model', *BioSystems*, vol. 5, pp. 187–196.

McCraty, R, Atkinson, M & Tomasino, D 2001, *Science of the heart: exploring the role of the heart in human performance*, HeartMath Research Center, HR Center, Boulder Creek, California.

McLean, J 2017, *'Embedding sustainability into organisational DNA: A story of complexity'*, Faculty of the Professions, Adelaide Business School, Doctor of Philosophy thesis, University of Adelaide, Adelaide.

Meadows, DH 2008, *Thinking in systems: a primer*, Chelsea Green Publishing, Boston

Meyer, W, Bryan, B, Lyle, G, McLean, J, Moon, T, Siebentritt, D, Summers, D & Wells, S 2013, *Adapted future landscapes – from aspiration to implementation*, National Climate Change Adaptation Research Foundation, Adelaide.

O'Fallon, T 2010, 'Developmental experiments in individual and collective movement to second tier', *Journal of Integral Theory & Practice*, vol. 5, no. 2. pp. 149–160.

O'Malley, E & Cebula, A 2015, *Your leadership edge: lead anytime, anywhere*, KLC Press, Wichita, Kansas.

Parks, SD 2005, *Leadership can be taught: a bold approach for a complex world*, Harvard Business School Press, Boston.

Rule, N 2014, *Snap-judgment science*, Association for Psychological Science, viewed 18 December 2019, <https://www.psychologicalscience.org/observer/snap-judgment-science>.

Schein, EH 1990, 'Organizational culture', *American Psychologist*, vol. 45, no. 2, pp. 109–119.

Scholtes, PR 1988, *The team handbook: how to use teams to improve quality*, Joiner Associates, Madison, WI.

Schwartz, J & Rock, D 2006, 'The neuroscience of leadership', *Strategy + Business*, no. 43.

Senge, P 1994, *The fifth discipline*, Doubleday, New York.

Sweeney, LB & Meadows, D 1995, *The systems thinking playbook*, Canada.

Symes, I 2014, *The flux report: building a resilient workforce in the face of flux*, Right Management, London, UK.

Tuff, G & Wunker, S 2014, *Beacons for business model innovation.* Deloitte, USA

Wahl, DC 2017, *[7 key questions about how to] participate appropriately in complex systems*, Medium, viewed 22 June 2019, <https://medium.com/age-of-awareness/how-can-we-participate-appropriately-in-complex-systems-aec17e74cd9f>.

Wells, S & McLean, J 2013, 'One way forward to beat the Newtonian habit with a complexity perspective on organisational change', *Systems*, vol. 1, no. 4, pp. 66–84.

Wells, S & McLean, J 2020, in press, 'Emergent organizational change: A living systems perspective', in GS Metcalf, H Deguchi & K Kijima (eds), *Handbook of systems sciences*, Springer, Singapore.

Wheatley, MJ 1999, *Leadership and the new science: Discovering order in a chaotic world*, 2nd edn, Berrett-Koehler, San Francisco.

Wood, AJ, & Beale, C 2019, *Starling murmurations: the science behind one of nature's greatest displays*, PhysOrg, viewed 7 December 2019, <https://phys.org/news/2019-02-starling-murmurations-science-nature-greatest.html>.

Zander, B & Zander, RS 2000, *The art of possibility: transforming professional and personal life*, Harvard Business School Press, Boston.

About the Author

Josie began her career as a financial analyst and corporate strategic planner in the automotive and finance industries. She has been fascinated by the intersection of strategy, people, process and change ever since.

In 1999, she commenced her executive coaching practice that extended into organisational cultural evolution by 2009. During that year Josie also received the global International Coach Federation President's 2009 Award for her contribution as a co-founder of the professional coaching industry in Australasia.

Josie's doctoral thesis involved her as an external change agent within a client organisation to understand how an organisation might transform itself to nurture people and planet– just like a person might – from the inside out.

She continues to work in the ambiguous space of adaptive learning and change within organisations and communities.

Increasingly her work is turning to teaching others what she has learned about complex challenges and how to move forward within them.

Josie continues to research and publish as a Visiting Research Fellow at the University of Adelaide's Yunus Social Business Centre and is also a co-founder on the global Climate Coaching Alliance initiative.